Man and Land in Peru

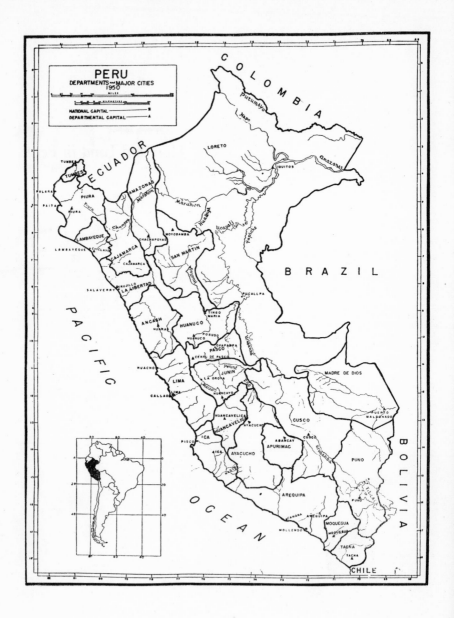

Man and Land in Peru

by Thomas R. Ford

University of Florida Press
Gainesville — 1955

A Univerity of Florida Press Book

Copyright, 1955, University of Florida

All Rights Reserved

Library of Congress Catalogue Card No. 55-9942

Printed by Convention Press, Jacksonville, Florida

Contents

v

Preface

MAN IS A SOCIAL ANIMAL, nearly all of his ac-
tivities being carried on through cooperative interaction with his fellow
human beings. It is through such interaction that basic human needs
—both group and individual—are met. Each society tends to repeat
cooperative activities which have proved successful in achieving given
ends, until eventually the processes become stabilized systems of actions
and relationships. It is to be recognized, of course, that different societies meet similar needs with quite dissimilar social systems. This fact
poses two questions of fundamental significance to the social scientist:
(1) Under what conditions do certain characteristic social forms develop? (2) What are the effects of the operation of different types of
systems upon the societies in which they are utilized?

In this study I have been primarily concerned with the social systems that develop around the utilization of agricultural lands. My
"laboratory" was the territory that is now Peru, a region admirably
suited for such a study because within it have operated radically different systems of land tenure and use. The indigenous inhabitants developed a highly organized and complex system of a type that we would
now call "collectivistic." In the sixteenth century, the Spanish con-
quistadores arrived and instituted their own "individualistic" system.
Today, four centuries later, the resulting chaos has still not been resolved, and both systems can still be found in operation.

I have attempted to trace the evolution of the contemporary land
system of Peru from pre-Inca days through the Colonial Period and the
Republic to mid-twentieth century. In each era I have described the

characteristic features of the system and its general social effects. Particular attention is given to the current critical problems of food production in Peru, relating them to the fundamental issues of land tenure and distribution.

It is only fitting that I should acknowledge some of the more outstanding debts of gratitude which I owe in connection with this book, even though it is impossible to list all who have aided in making it possible. The basic research undertaking was made possible through a Cordell Hull Fellowship that was established by Mr. and Mrs. Jesse Jones at Vanderbilt University in honor of that eminent statesman. Substantial aid was also provided in the form of a travel grant awarded by the United States Office of Education. Many persons in Peru gave of their time, energy, and experience in the furthering of the research during my stay in 1949-1950. I can only mention, as being among the most helpful, the following: Mr. John R. Neale, able Director of the Servicio Cooperativo Inter-Americano de Producción de Alimentos; Sr. Pedro Pérez Palacio, Chief of the Division of Statistical and Economic Studies of SCIPA; Dr. Leoncio M. Palacios, Professor of Economic Geography at the University of San Marcos and Director of the Department of Labor and Social Statistics, National Bureau of Statistics of Peru; and Mr. Roy E. Westley, Agricultural Attaché of the United States Embassy in Peru. I am particularly indebted to Ing. Miguel Castro, not only for the unmatched professional advice that he was able to offer from his experience as an agricultural economist for SCIPA and as an agriculturist in his own right, but also for his numerous personal acts of courtesy and kindness.

At Vanderbilt University, where the study was originally presented as a doctoral dissertation, various individuals assisted during the different stages of project planning and execution. Among them must be mentioned Professors T. Lynn Smith, Olen Leonard, Wayland J. Hayes, Emilio Willems, Alexander Marchant, Reynold E. Carlson, and Abbott Ferriss.

My wife, Harriet Lowrey Ford, assumed the major burdens of preparing the bibliography and index, in addition to editing, reading proof, and typing more drafts of the manuscript than either of us likes to reflect upon.

The author alone is, of course, responsible for the views and opinions expressed herein, none of which should be construed as necessarily carrying the sanction or endorsement of any of the individuals or organizations mentioned above.

T. R. F.

Montgomery, Alabama
1954

Introduction

PERU IS NOT ONE LAND, but many. It is a land of jungles and mountains, rivers and deserts, fertile valleys and barren rocks. Its people are selvatic tribesmen who hunt and fish and reap the wild harvest of the Amazon rain forests. They are also sturdy Indian agriculturists and herdsmen—descendants of the once mighty Incas and their subjects—inhabitants of the lofty, wind-swept Andes. They are bronze-skinned mestizo miners, policemen, taxi drivers, and city laborers. They are white Spanish-American lawyers and doctors; bankers and entrepreneurs; career officers in the armed forces; priests and politicians. The people of Peru are all these things and more. And their cultures, coexisting, span ten thousand years of human history.

It is somewhat difficult—at least to North Americans—to think of Peru as a modern nation. Its rich past looms too large, overshadowing the present: the fabulous Inca Empire; Pizarro's daring conquest; the lavish colonial era; the winning of independence under the gallant and idealistic leadership of San Martín and Bolívar. But of the republic, of contemporary Peru, little is heard. Even the travel books hark ever back to the ruins of bygone ages, neglecting the present except, perhaps, for reports on night life in Lima and the quality of the hotels. So the typical tourist makes the rounds of bars and ruins, visits the "quaint" Indian fairs, and returns home, oblivious to the truly momentous social drama currently being enacted.

What is happening in Peru today is not easy to describe, because it is not a simple occurrence. It is a complex metamorphosis. To put it briefly, and inadequately, the nation is moving toward industrialization.

1

The industrialization process, as Europe and North America have learned, is complicated enough in itself. In Peru, though, there is an additional facet to the problem in that an extraordinary range of economic and technological levels is involved: preagricultural, collective agrarian, feudal, subsistence-farming, and commercial. And each level supports a separate system of social organization, cultural behavior, and beliefs. Peru is, therefore, more than a single nation undergoing the radical transformation produced by industry. It represents a changing world. Therein lies its significance, its profound drama.

Had a true synthesis of Spanish and native cultures been achieved during the centuries following the conquest of Peru, the current situation faced by the nation would be decidedly different. But such was not the case; the social and cultural differences were of such a nature that no easy merger was possible. The Indian society was collectivistic and highly regimented, functioning to produce the greatest possible agricultural yields from limited land resources. The role of the individual was to serve his appointed function in the system to which he was subordinate and upon which his existence depended. On the other hand, the Spanish colonial economy was based, in practice if not in theory, on the principles of individual enterprise and private property. The Indian felt he benefited himself by serving society; the Spaniard felt he benefited society by serving himself. The Indian sought security; the conquistador sought prestige. The Indian valued the land because it was his home, his life; the Spaniard valued the land as a symbol of status. In the end the system of the conqueror prevailed, but that of the vanquished endured. The elaborate social structure of the Inca Empire was, of course, destroyed, but the Indian way of life persevered inasmuch as it remained intimately dependent upon the soil. The Spanish landowner, content with the mere fact of ownership (together with a goodly share of what his Indian laborers might produce), was willing to leave the natives otherwise relatively undisturbed. It was a quasi-feudal system erected on a collectivist base. One is reminded of the Spanish colonial churches in Cuzco which were built directly upon foundations of Inca walls.

The uneasy equilibrium attained through this symbiotic relationship was able to persist for several centuries. Even the political revolution through which national independence was obtained failed to upset the balance. But the process of industrialization shakes any agrarian system to its very roots, and Peru has proved no exception. New patterns of social and economic organization are being adopted, new values are being accepted; both feudalism and agrarian collectivism seem doomed to disappear. The disturbances are felt throughout the nation.

There is always the tendency to treat such social changes in terms of impersonal forces and shifting institutions, forgetting that ultimately they must be reckoned in terms of upset lives. Restlessly moving individuals and families, uprooted by forces which they vainly seek to comprehend, are the surface manifestations of deeper social tides. The more stolid accept their unknown prospects resignedly. The resentful would seek to stop the inexorable process, but to give it fight they must give it form. Like so many other agricultural peoples in similar positions, they define their ills in terms of their keenest hurt—the broken ties with the land. So the remedy they seek is with the land system; a vain hope, perhaps, but nonetheless real. Men have died for wilder dreams, and uncounted thousands have died for this particular one.

It is for these reasons that the subject of man-land relations—the interrelated complexes of property rights and land distribution—was chosen as the focus for this study of the changing order in Peru. There were other reasons, of course, both academic and expediential. An all-embracing study of the multiple and ramified changes occurring in the Peruvian sociocultural system would be of inestimable value to both theoretical and applied social science. It would also require the work of a number of social scientists over a considerable period of time. Only rarely is a research institution or government willing to bear the costs of such an ambitious undertaking. As a consequence, more modest objectives must be defined which can be achieved with the available resources of time and money, not to mention talent. In the light of these considerations, too, a study of man-land relations seems to offer a logical approach to a wider understanding of the changing society of Peru.

The basic assumption of this work is that the man-land systems of Peru—the patterns of land distribution and tenure practices—have been in the past and still are directly and functionally related to the manifold sets of other fundamental variables that shape the whole of Peruvian social and cultural life. These other sets of variables include the factors of natural environment, population structure and processes, social organization, technology, and cultural values and attitudes. As a corollary, the changing forms of man-land relations reflect and produce changes in other sets of interrelated factors. The sensitivity of man-land relations patterns as a gauge of change in the structural whole undoubtedly is heavily dependent upon the economy of the nation being studied. In the case of Peru, where the economy has for countless generations been based upon agriculture and for the most part still is, the changes in social and cultural patterns developed around the land are both sensitive and reliable indexes of changes occurring in the larger sociocultural web of which they are a part. But like all indexes, this one must be interpreted. Admittedly, some of the interpretations transcend their empirical references, and deduction degenerates into speculation. Wherever possible, though, documentation has been provided, and speculation indicated as such.

In the limited time available for this study it was possible to obtain detailed data on only two of the previously mentioned sets of variables to which the systems of man-land relations are functionally related. These two, on natural environment and population, have been presented in a brief preliminary chapter because they are not only helpful but to some extent necessary to an understanding of the discussions which follow.

1.

The Land and the People

EVEN TO THE MOST CASUAL OBSERVER of the Peruvian countryside it is clear that the forces of natural environment are of tremendous importance in their influence upon many aspects of social and economic operation. The striking contrasts of deserts, mountains, and jungles—all to be encountered within a few longitudinal degrees—are truly impressive. At first glance, the stringent limitations imposed by the peculiar geography of the nation might appear directly responsible for the complex social structure through which a comparatively small amount of arable land is distributed among many thousands of agricultural families. On reflection, though, it is to be recalled that through the years from pre-Inca society to the present day, the systems of man-land relations have undergone radical alterations, while the geographic factors have remained relatively unchanged. Essentially, the role of natural environment has been more or less that of a constant in the agrarian equation, influential yet relatively invariant. The fact that geographic factors do enter into the network of relationships requires that they be described and analyzed in terms of their features and effects.

THE GEOGRAPHIC SETTING

First, it might be pointed out that Peru is not so small a country as it is usually thought to be. In South America only Brazil and Argentina exceed it in area. It is roughly comparable in size to the entire southeastern region of the United States, comprising Virginia, North Carolina,

5

South Carolina, Florida, Tennessee, Alabama, Mississippi, Arkansas, and Louisiana, a total area of slightly less than half a million square miles. Yet, of this expanse it is estimated that only about 3,700,000 acres are cultivated, or barely more than 1 per cent of the total area. This is roughly one-third of the cultivated acreage of Louisiana, which has the least of any of the aforementioned southeastern states. Fortunately, much of the uncultivated area in Peru is suitable for grazing, so agriculture is supplemented by ranching industries. Together, agricultural and ranching enterprises employed nearly two-thirds of the economically active population of the nation in 1940.[1]

With regard to its natural features, the country is usually considered in terms of three broad divisions: the coast, the sierra, and the selva, or montaña. (Fig. 1.) In reality, each of these broad regions is composed of various subregions, so that the three-divisional scheme is a gross oversimplification. The wide range of altitude in the sierra, for example, produces a great variety of natural environmental phenomena. The montaña is composed of a "high" selva and a "low" selva, which differ considerably in their physical characteristics. A closer look at each of the regions should help to clarify their differences.

The coastal region of Peru is a desert strip extending from three degrees south of the equator southeastward to the border of Chile. Its greatest width, about seventy-five miles, is in the north, which section also supports more vegetation—in the form of xerophytic shrub—than does the south. The strip narrows considerably in its southern reaches, with spurs of the cordillera frequently extending to the sea. The altitude of the coast varies from sea level to a more or less arbitrarily established 1,500 meters, where it merges with the western sierra.

The extreme aridity of the coast is due to a coincidence of factors. Chief among them are the Andean ranges, which rob any southeast winds of their moisture, and the Peruvian, or Humboldt, Current which, by lowering the sea temperature below that of the land, generally prevents rain from the west.[2] Only the fifty-two rivers that empty into the Pacific save the coast from being almost totally barren, and most of these are dry during the late winter months. From these rivers come the irrigation waters that make fertile slightly more than a million acres of cul-

tivated coastal fields. It is this area, or a part of it, which sustains practically all the commercial farming of cotton and sugar cane in Peru.

FIGURE 1

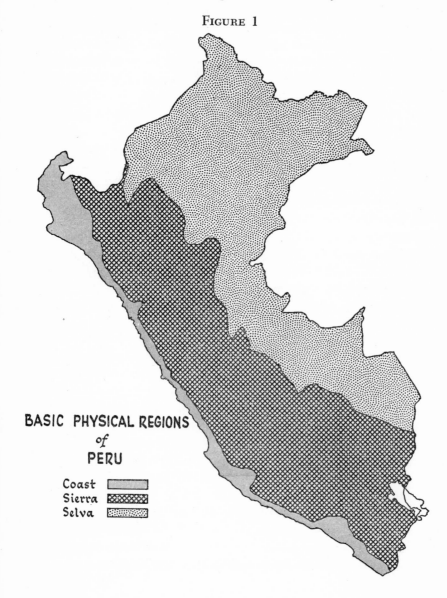

BASIC PHYSICAL REGIONS
of
PERU

Coast
Sierra
Selva

These fertile valleys, a bare 5 per cent of the total coastal area, are true oases, both physically and economically.

The sierra, as has been noted, is not one but many regions, upon whose division there is no complete agreement. Some geographers prefer a vertical classification, using altitude as the chief criterion of distinction.[3] Others point out the significance of latitude and other factors which complicate the effect of altitude, and so, applying different criteria, come out with different divisions.[4]

The topography of the region is, of course, extremely irregular except in the flat intermontane valleys or basins. The mountain ranges do not have the clear continuity of the Andes farther to the north in Ecuador and Colombia, but are disconnected and present a complex pattern. In the extreme south, bordering on Bolivia, there are two ranges which appear to unite in the so-called "Vilcanota Knot," which forms part of the rim of the Lake Titicaca basin.[5] From this point three ranges emerge toward the north. The westernmost parallels the coast. A second, and rather complicated, cordillera forms the central chain, while the third, of slightly less altitude, borders the montaña. Between the central and western ranges flows the Apurímac River; between the central and eastern ranges, the Urubamba. The valleys of these two rivers offer rich agricultural zones. In addition, there are numerous smaller transverse valleys, called *quebradas*, which are suitable for farming.

After separate and intricate peregrinations over the southern part of Peru the three cordilleras appear to unite again at Cerro de Pasco in the central region about one degree north of the latitude of Lima. This is an area famed for both its wealth and its variety of minerals. Here, also, five great rivers have their origins: the Marañon and the Huallaga, which flow to the north; the Pachitea and the Perené, which run eastward to join the great Ucayali that flows into the Amazon; and the Mantaro, which flows southward between the western and central ranges.

From Pasco three more general ranges emerge, the western chain shortly dividing into the Cordillera Negra and the Cordillera Blanca, between which lies the Callejón de Huaylas. The central range serves as the dividing line between the Marañon and Huallaga watersheds. The eastern range—or, more accurately, ranges—diminishes in altitude and appears to merge with the central cordillera in the northern latitudes of the country.

Although the longitudinal and transverse valleys of the sierra are by far the most suitable areas for cultivation, some tillage of the mountain slopes is practiced, but generally with poor results. More frequently the mountainsides are used for grazing wherever there is sufficient natural vegetation. Except on the westernmost slopes, rainfall is abundant in the sierra, but its utility is diminished by its seasonal nature. In much of the region periods of too much water alternate with periods of too little water, since reservoirs and irrigation facilities are generally lacking to smooth the distribution. The rugged nature of the terrain has been a constant handicap to mechanization and transportation, retarding the development of commercial farming of the types found on the coast. To a great extent agriculture in the region has remained geared to a subsistence economy, with the great part of the produce, primarily potatoes and grains, being consumed in the area itself.

The montaña is of no great relevance to the matters of prime consideration in this treatise, but a brief geographical description will help to explain why it is not. First, even though the region constitutes some 60 per cent of the total area of Peru, its contribution to the national economy is practically nil. The "high" selva, frequently referred to as the *ceja de montaña* (literally, "eyebrow of the montaña"), is somewhat mountainous, with frequent *quebradas* adding to the irregularity of its topography. The rainfall in the area is heavy and the vegetation lush. For more than a century this section has been periodically proclaimed the logical center of future colonization and, as such, the locale of a "new" Peru. To date, however, geographic isolation combined with primitive transportation facilities has prevented the realization of the dream except in a few limited locations. It is in this region that the coca plantations flourish, furnishing the sierra Indians with the cocaine-yielding leaves that sustain their every activity.

The "low" selva is tropical rainforest—hot, humid, and subject to seasonal floods in many parts. The population consists of aboriginal tribes that were never subjugated either by the highland Incas or by the Spaniards. They have dwelt in relative isolation throughout the centuries, subsisting largely through hunting, fishing, and gathering wild foods. The area is primarily noted for such products as lumber, rubber, balata (a resinous gum used in varnishes), tagua (vegetable ivory), and barbasco, or cube (a root used in insecticides). The most recent boom in the economy of the area occurred during World War II but subsided with the development of synthetics and the reopening of more accessible regions after hostilities ceased. Because natural production has generally been sufficiently high to meet market demands, most of the products mentioned above have never been systematically cultivated in the area.

Until some means is found of clearing the land cheaply and considerable improvement is made in transportation facilities, it seems extremely doubtful that the economic potential of the montaña will be developed to any extent. Thus, even though agriculture is practiced in various parts of the high selva, its net contribution to the national economy, except for the coca plantations, is relatively unimportant.

THE PERUVIAN POPULATION

Unlike the natural environment, population factors cannot be treated as relative constants in the consideration of the man-land relational system of Peru. Their functional relationship with land tenure and distribution is one of reciprocity, of influencing and being influenced in turn. In many respects their effects are indirect and are complicated by the introduction of numerous other factors. A detailed analysis of these complex relationships is not intended here, but rather the provision of some basic demographic data necessary to the understanding of the relationships that are later discussed.

In 1940, after a sixty-four-year lapse, a general census of the Peruvian population was taken, providing much information on matters which previously had been objects of estimate and sheer conjecture. Despite their many inadequacies the official census tabulations provide by far the most reliable materials on the demographic characteristics of the Peruvian population at the present time.

The size of the Peruvian population as actually enumerated in 1940 was 6,207,947. Calculations of known omissions, however, served to raise the total estimate for the census year to more than 7,000,000. According to more recent government estimates, the mid-century population of the nation exceeded 8,000,000. If these figures are accepted, the population of Peru is the fifth largest among Latin American nations, ranking after Brazil, Mexico, Argentina, and Colombia, in that order.

An examination of the distribution of the people shows, as might logically be expected, concentrations in the basins and *quebradas* of the sierra and in the verdant valleys crossing the coastal desert. According to census computations, 62 per cent of the population was located in the sierra, while 25 per cent of the total resided on the coast and the remaining 13 per cent was located in the selva. The census classified nearly two-thirds of the population as "rural" in 1940, a figure that can be considered most conservative, since all residents of the capitals of minor civil divisions were automatically considered "urban" in 1940, as were persons who lived in towns larger than the mean population of such capitals. Since the average population of capital cities of this nature was only 2,013, it seems obvious that a large portion of the "urban" category could be considered so only nominally.[6]

Racial intermixture has taken place to such a considerable extent in Peru that census officials completely despaired of distinguishing whites from mestizos in 1940, and included them in a single category. Enumerators, however, did make a distinction between mestizos and Indians, although their criteria for doing so are by no means clear. From a cultural standpoint, some mestizos are Indians and so consider themselves. On the other hand, many of the most completely occidentalized members of Peruvian "white" society can refer to themselves and most of their friends as "we *cholos*," as they frequently do in jest or in political passion, without distorting the biological fact. By whatever means used, the census classified approximately 53 per cent of the population as white and mestizo and about 46 per cent as Indian. The only other racial categories listed, as shown in Table 1, were Oriental and Negro, which together constituted barely more than 1 per cent of the population.

The comparative data on racial structure from the censuses of 1876 and 1940 shown in Table 1 lend statistical support to the view that the process of mestizage has accelerated considerably in recent decades. But

TABLE 1
RACIAL COMPOSITION OF THE PERUVIAN
POPULATION, 1876 AND 1940

Racial Classification	Population 1876		Population 1940	
	Number	Percentage	Number	Percentage
White and mestizo	1,040,652	38.55	3,283,360	52.89
Indian	1,554,678	57.60	2,847,196	45.86
Oriental	51,186	1.90	45,945	.68
Negro	52,588	1.95	29,054	.47
Unknown	2	——	6,412	.10
Total	2,699,106	100.00	6,211,967	100.00

Source: Censo nacional, . . .1940, I, clxxx.

it is to be noticed that the Indian population, despite its proportionate loss of 12 per cent in terms of its contribution to the total, increased numerically by more than a million between 1876 and 1940. Negroes and Orientals, on the other hand, decreased numerically as well as proportionately.

The sierra remains the stronghold of the Indian way of life, as is borne out by the fact that only in the nine departments of that region does the Indian population still remain a majority element. A fairly reliable guide to the acculturation process which has accompanied racial intermixture is seen in the spread of the Spanish language. In 1940 the non-Spanish-speaking population outnumbered the Spanish-speaking group in only seven departments. Yet this does not mean that Spanish is the most frequently used idiom. As shown in Table 2, the number of persons speaking either Quechua or Aymara was greater than the number who knew only Spanish. Approximately one person of every six in 1940 could speak both Spanish and one of the Indian languages. Quechua, however, is far more widely spoken than Aymara, the latter language being utilized by less than 5 per cent of the population localized in the Lake Titicaca region and the department of Puno.

One of the more significant demographic guides to social processes is the age and sex composition of a population. The age-sex pyramid of Peru has a wide base and a low apex, typical of a nation with both birth

TABLE 2

LANGUAGES SPOKEN BY VARIOUS PROPORTIONS
OF THE PERUVIAN POPULATION, 1940

LANGUAGES	PERCENTAGE OF POPULATION SPEAKING
Spanish only	46.7
Spanish and one or more foreign languages	1.7
Spanish and an Indian language	16.6
Indian language only (chiefly Quechua and Aymara)	35.0
	100.0

Source: Censo nacional, . . . 1940, I, 163, cuadro 46.

and death rates high. (Fig. 2.) The relative youthfulness of the population is striking. In 1940 over half the population was under 20 years of age, with a mean age of barely over 24.[7] This average would be lowered even further, at least temporarily, through the elimination of conditions responsible for the extremely high infant mortality rate. The sex ratio of 97.7 (males per 100 females) for the nation as a whole reveals a preponderance of females that seems to be accounted for only by a relatively higher mortality rate for males. Strong support is given this assumption by the fact that the excess of females develops only after the twentieth year of life and becomes especially marked after the age 50.

Because the registration of vital statistics in Peru is far from complete, although it is legally required, census data probably offer a more accurate picture of natural increase than do records of births and deaths. The rate of natural increase is exceptionally high despite an elevated annual death toll. The reason for this phenomenon is simply that the birth rate is so much higher than the death rate. The calculated rate of population increase between 1876 and 1940 was approximately 2 per cent annually, which meant that the population increased more than 125 per cent in the sixty-four years between censuses.[8] Relatively little of this increase could be attributed to immigration.

The health hazards of life in Peru, however, are revealed in the mortality statistics. Even with deficient registration, the average crude death rate over the ten-year period from 1930 to 1940 was 17 per

FIGURE 2

POPULATION DISTRIBUTED BY AGE AND SEX PERU AND THE UNITED STATES, 1940

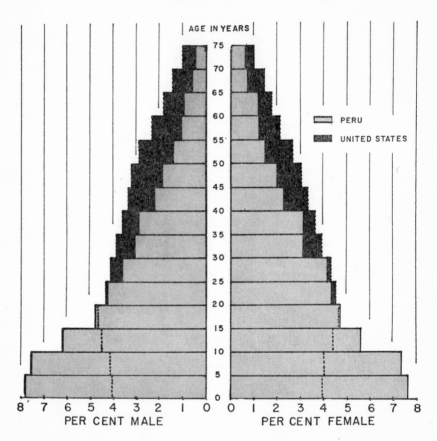

1,000. The comparable rate in the United States during the same period was slightly more than 11 per 1,000, despite more complete registration and a considerably higher proportion of the population in the older groups. The crude death rate in Peru dropped from 13.2 in 1940 to 11.7 in 1950, with even lower rates recorded during some of the intervening years;[9] but it is to be remembered that these figures are based on registered deaths and that the registration process in far from complete.

A more sensitive index than crude death rates is provided by the infant mortality rate, which, in Peru, ranged during the decade of 1941-1950 from a high of 130.6 infant deaths per 1,000 live births at the beginning of the period to a low of 93.7 at the end.[10] This was roughly three times as great as the infant death rate in the United States for the same ten-year span, and about five times the comparable rate in New Zealand. These figures mean that considerably more than 10 per cent of the infants whose births are recorded die before they reach the age of 1 year. It seems a safe speculation that the death rates of the unrecorded segment are even higher. The tremendous loss of young life is further emphasized by the fact that nearly half of the annual recorded deaths in the nation occur in the group under 5 years of age.[11] In 1949, for instance, some 85,406 persons died in Peru; of these, 21,736—more than a fourth—were less than a year old, while 39,447, or more than 46 per cent, were under 5 years of age.[12]

As already observed, high birth rates in Peru more than compensate for population losses suffered because of generally unfavorable health and medical facilities. During the period from 1930 to 1940 the crude birth rate computed for the nation was 31 per 1,000, a figure which more adequate registration would undoubtedly have raised substantially. The rate during the following decade fluctuated around 25 per 1,000, although the 1950 figure recorded was 30.3. The highest rate recorded in the United States during the same period was 25.7 in the postwar year of 1947. But a more reliable measure of fertility than the crude birth rate is the fertility ratio, based upon the number of living children under 5 years of age per 1,000 women aged 15-49. The ratio for Peru in 1940 was one of the highest in the Western Hemisphere, 655. For the United States in the same year the fertility ratio was only 281. The accuracy of this remarkable figure for Peru seems substantiated by other census information revealing that two-thirds of the women over 15 years of age had borne 1 or more children.[13] The average number of children born per mother was approximately 5, but less than two-thirds of those born alive were still living at the time of the enumeration.

Other demographic clues to an understanding of social and economic processes in Peru are provided by information on the size and direction of migration flow. Such data, unfortunately, are limited, but internal movements may be inferred from departmental breakdowns of census materials on age and sex structure, place of birth, and place of residence at the time of the enumeration. In Table 3 the residential distribution of the 1940 population is given, classified by region of birth. The principal inference that can be made from this table is that there has been a significant migration from the sierra to other regions, particularly to the coast. Migrants from the coast and the selva to the sierra, however, contribute in only a small degree to the population of the mountain region.

TABLE 3
PERUVIAN POPULATION RESIDING IN SELECTED REGIONS IN
1940, CLASSIFIED BY REGION OF BIRTH

PLACE OF RESIDENCE 1940	PERCENTAGES OF POPULATION BORN IN SPECIFIED REGIONS				
	Coast	Sierra	Selva	Foreign	Total
Coast	85.66	11.66	0.37	2.31	100.00
Sierra	1.34	98.25	0.12	0.29	100.00
Selva	1.05	1.94	97.17	0.84	101.00

Source: Censo nacional, . . . 1940, I, clxiii.

There are several features of importance that are not revealed in this regional tabulation. One of these is that the migration represented as being to the coast is in reality largely to the two cities of Lima and Callao. This is evident from two other sets of data provided by the census. First, not all the coastal provinces show a net increase in population through migration, and second, more than half of the persons enumerated outside of their native departments were residing either in the department of Lima or in the constitutional province of Callao.[14]

The selective character of the coastal migration is revealed by a comparative analysis of the sex ratios of rural sierra departments and the urban coastal departments. As shown in Table 4, the former departments show a marked lack of males, while the latter reveal, with one exception, a preponderance of males. It is quite possible that these figures have captured a temporary condition of seasonal migration of farm labor, but there is no easy way to check this possibility. The principal clue to the nature of intraregional migration is furnished by the data which show the nativity by departments of the enumerated population. In 1940 only eight of the twenty-four departments had received sufficient numbers of migrants to replace the losses of native sons and daughters to other departments. (Callao, a constitutional province, is listed as

TABLE 4

SEX RATIOS IN FIVE MOST URBAN COASTAL DEPARTMENTS
AND FIVE MOST RURAL SIERRA DEPARTMENTS, 1940

URBAN DEPARTMENTS	PER CENT URBAN	SEX RATIO	RURAL DEPARTMENTS	PER CENT RURAL	SEX RATIO
Callao (prov.)	99	110	Puno	87	95
Lima	76	105	Apurímac	86	92
Arequipa	59	92	Cajamarca	86	92
Tacna	53	116	Huancavelica	85	92
Lambayeque	51	110	Huánuco	81	99

Source: Censo nacional, . . . 1940, I, 48-51, cuadro 5; 90-93, cuadro 19.

a department.) These departments were Callao, Cuzco, Lambayeque, La Libertad, Lima, Loreto, Madre de Dios, and Tacna. Two of these are principally in the selva, Loreto and Madre de Dios. Cuzco is a sierra department, and the province of Callao can be considered entirely coastal. The remainder lie partly in the sierra and partly on the coast, but most of the larger cities are in the coastal sections.

Common sense and data from other countries suggest that the bulk of the migrants are young adults. It should therefore be expected that the departments receiving migrants should show higher proportions of individuals in the economically productive age group (20-59 years) than is true for the nation as a whole. This assumption is borne out by the data, with the exception of the selva department of Loreto, indicating that migration to the selva should be separately interpreted. The sex selectivity of the migration is also borne out by the fact that all eight departments with net gains of migrants showed proportions of males in the economically productive age group that were higher than the national proportion. Unfortunately for the cause of pat interpretations, the populations of several departments that had lost migrants also showed this characteristic.

One hesitates to draw any hard and fast conclusions on the basis of such materials. But it does not seem too venturesome to point out a few features of internal migration that seem indicated and substantiated by the little information that is available. First, the sierra contributes the largest number and proportion of interregional migrants, most of whom go to the coast and particularly to Lima. Second, these migrants are predominantly males in the economically productive age bracket. Third, both the interregional and intraregional migrants tend to move to the cities, especially to the larger cities. Fourth, there is some migration to the selva which appears to be of an altogether different character from the other internal movements in that it is not so selective of males. The observations of the American anthropologist Bernard Mishkin suggest that this may be a movement of families to new agricultural lands in the high selva.[15]

Some further comprehension of characteristics of the Peruvian population may be gained from the census materials on religion and education. With respect to the former, suffice it to say that 98.5 per cent of the population is, at least nominally, Roman Catholic. Even to the most casual observer, however, it is obvious that many characteristics of indigenous religions have been syncretized with the Christian elements. The tacit acceptance of this intermixture by the Roman Catholic Church undoubtedly contributed to the rapid acceptance and spread of Christian ritual and theology among the Indians. The powerful influence of religion on the attitudes and actions of Peruvians of all kinds and social levels is readily apparent, but at the same time is of such a diverse and complex nature as to defy any facile analysis.

Educational data may be interpreted more easily. If formal education is a major factor in the acculturation process, as is commonly thought, the persistence of ethnic differences in Peru can certainly be explained in large part by the lack of widespread educational programs. In 1940, 60 per cent of the enumerated population over 6 years of age had received no formal school instruction. Of the 40 per cent who had received such instruction, 61 per cent had been limited to an "elementary" education (considered as the first three years of elementary school) or less. Another 28 per cent had reached the "primary" level (fourth or fifth years), while only 11 per cent had advanced beyond the fifth grade. On the whole, males had received more formal education than females—a typical Latin American characteristic—the proportion of instructed males to females being 3 to 2. In the upper educational brackets (university or superior education) the ratio increased to 5 to 1. This increase, however, was doubtless due to the inclusion of military and police schools among the institutions of "superior" education. With rare exceptions, the greatest lack of formal education was to be found in the departments with the highest proportions of Indian populations. The more urban coastal departments, with the highest proportions of whites, showed the greatest average amounts of formal schooling.

The findings of the 1940 census with respect to education prompted the Peruvian government to launch an intensive educational campaign, the full results of which will have to be determined by the next census. It is not difficult to understand why the provision of formal education for the citizenry is considered in many quarters to be one of the primary problems faced by the nation.

This brief sketch of natural environmental features and population characteristics of the Peruvian nation should suffice to introduce some of the basic factors which are functionally related to the man-land systems at the present time. Several important points should be kept in mind for the later analysis of these relationships.

First, tremendous natural barriers have always obstructed, and will continue to obstruct, the development of Peruvian agriculture. The scarcity of cultivable land imposes restrictions that can be overcome only through methods requiring tremendous capital investments. The altitude and topography of the sierra not only preclude the utilization of modern farm machinery in many regions but also raise transportation costs so that an investment is not economical at the present time even where such equipment could be used.

Second, there is increasing population pressure upon a restricted amount of agricultural land. The population of Peru has doubled in the last half century. Continuing at its present rate of increase, it will redouble in the next half. The spread of modern medicine and sanitary engineering attending industrialization will doubtless increase the rate, at least temporarily, and serious problems of providing for the increased millions must be met.

Third, heavy pressure on the land has already served to stimulate migration, particularly from the sierra region. Most of it is toward the cities of the coast, but some of it is toward the eastern lowlands, long heralded as the cradle of a new prosperity. But until the new prosperity develops, radical disturbances must almost inevitably occur as the flow of migration becomes heavier.

The factors of geography and population are of considerable moment in their influence upon social developments, particularly upon the systems of man-land relations. Even so, they are not determinative factors in themselves; they account only partly for the shaping of social forms and the development of new relationships. Other sets of factors are of equal importance; yet they cannot be so easily isolated and analyzed. For that matter, their interaction has been of such a nature that little purpose would be served by their separate treatment. As an alternative, an effort has been made in this work to trace briefly the evolution of current man-land relations with emphasis on the historical perspective rather than the panoramic view.

2.

The Evolution of Man-Land Relational Systems in Peru

THE CONTEMPORARY AGRARIAN SITUATION of Peru is virtually unfathomable without a general understanding of the historical processes which have produced it. The evolution has been highly complex, but at the same time fairly clearly, and at times dramatically, divided into distinct stages. The lack of written records leaves our knowledge of the earliest periods of pre-Inca history quite deficient, but after the rise of the Inca nation the epochs are more easily perceived, the dividing lines more sharply drawn. The clearest line of all is that drawn by the sword of Francisco Pizarro in the sands of the Isla del Gallo when he boldly challenged his men to step across and join him in the conquest of Peru. Almost equally tangible is the end of the colonial period, punctuated by the establishment of the new republic in 1821 under the banners of San Martín, "the Liberator," and Bolívar, "the Protector."

Changes reflected in the kaleidoscope of Peruvian political history have been much more rapid than those of the profound social processes, however. Even the establishment of the Inca Empire was more a matter of integrating existing social forms under a common superstructure than of a fundamental reorganizational process. Nor did the shattering Spanish conquest completely alter traditional patterns of social behavior and technology. For that matter, there were probably thousands of native inhabitants who were completely unaware of the change from colonial to independent national government, at least for a while. It made little

21

difference in their lives. And even today, there are remote sections of Peru where one feels closer in time to the Incas or to the colonial era than to the rapidly encroaching industrial civilization of the twentieth century.

Man-land relations have, of course, undergone manifold changes throughout the various stages of Peruvian history. But the alterations have not proceeded either uniformly or steadily, and in general they have tended to lag considerably behind political transformations. Some features have remained basically the same for more than half a millennium; others have altered radically within the twentieth century. To obtain a clearer idea of the evolutionary process, the principal characteristics of the man-land relational system during each of the major historical periods will be briefly sketched.

THE PRE-INCA PERIOD

All the pre-Inca cultures may be considered as a unit, because there is insufficient knowledge of their social organizations to justify a more detailed analysis. Most of our information about the numerous cultures that preceded the development of the Inca Empire has been gathered from archaeological materials and, to a considerably lesser extent, folklore. In general, it is as fragmentary as the potsherds from which the archaeologists have drawn their inferences, requiring considerable imagination for the construction of a meaningful whole. Probably because of the leeway granted in filling in vacancies, the amount of disagreement over the classifications and sequences of various local cultures is tremendous.

It seems fairly well-established that at some very early period—no one knows how far back—the inhabitants of present-day Peruvian territory were organized in small kinship units called *ayllus*. There is no agreement among antiquarians as to the exact nature of the *ayllu*. Some have described it as a matriarchal and matrilineal clan possessing totemic beliefs.[1] This concept has been challenged by later anthropologists in respect to all the characteristics claimed.[2]

There is no reason to assume that there was any uniform structure of the *ayllus*. It seems evident that they were relatively small locality groups, and it is not unreasonable to suppose that kinship ties were strong under such circumstances.

Bautista Saavedra, a Bolivian sociologist, conjectured that the initial bonds of blood relationship which held the *ayllu* together were gradually replaced by sentiments of agrarian solidarity.[3] As the *ayllus* increased in size, they tended to subdivide into different locality groups, but the various subgroups remained bound to each other by kinship and common interests. The tribes thus constituted maintained a territorial community with specific areas assigned to each subunit for use by its members.[4] The total land area of a tribe was called the *marca,* which presents a rather curious linguistic coincidence noted by Cunow in that the almost identical word *mark* had the same meaning among the Germanic tribes.[5]

With regard to the actual apportionment of lands within the various tribal units, we can only speculate from what was later practiced during the Inca period. Evidence suggests, however, that the Incas did not greatly distort the basic patterns of earlier times. Deducing from the general practices of a later day, it would appear that there was no concept of private ownership of the land. Rather, the land belonged to the tribe, and each family head was allotted a portion, the size of the allotment being governed by the size of the family. The fields were probably worked in common, or with a system of mutual aid, but each family received the harvest of its own plot.[6] There is also some evidence that plots were reassigned annually, although it is quite likely that the same families received rights to the same lands every year or at least until the structure of the family altered through births, marriages, or deaths. Undoubtedly there were variations from tribe to tribe, but the most significant, and apparently most common, feature was that individuals were not owners of the land. They simply received the right to till it and reap the harvest from it during their lifetime.

Through the course of centuries social structures of the pre-Inca peoples became more extended and complex. This was due to either natural growth or conquests, or to a combination of the two. The possible stages of development suggested by Philip Means are plausible, if not subject to proof, and are worthy of consideration.[7] The small *ayllu,* according to Means, was probably ruled by an elected head (*sinchi*) who served in times or crisis. As the tribal population and area grew larger, forming an *"ayllu* state," the chief executive's position became permanent and inherited. The executive was called the *curaca.* Organization of various of these smaller states into a compound nation required a more complex governing structure, resulting in the development of a feudal type of state such as that of the Incas.

The existence of extensive nations prior to the rise of the Inca Empire is largely to be inferred from the knowledge that there were distinguishable cultural systems that coexisted over a wide area. It does not seem likely that such widespread conformity as apparently prevailed at various periods could have occurred without the development of the systematic contacts which a social superstructure could have provided.

The most extensive culture prior to the Inca was that known as late Tiahuanaco. It was preceded by a variety of less extensive cultures that developed in separate valleys of the coast and in different regions of the sierra. There is no complete agreement as to either their chronology or their domain. The German archaeologist Max Uhle maintained that coastal cultures tended to spread to the sierra.[8] The late Peruvian archaeologist Julio Tello contended that exactly the reverse occurred, the sierra being the true cradle of the great cultures.[9] Means advanced the theory that cultures could have developed independently and concurrently in both regions, a view which is widely accepted at the present time.[10] Archaeological evidence, at least, substantiates the fact that separate and distinct cultures existed contemporaneously in different sections of both the coast and the sierra. It appears also that, after the development of cultural and possibly social homogeneity of the inhabitants of most of present-day Peruvian territory, there was a period of dispersion into smaller elements. An approximate chronology of major cultures which have been distinguished, and their locales, are shown in Table 5.

It is to be kept in mind that our knowledge of early life in Peru is largely derived from material artifacts, a poor source of information on such matters as social and political organization. What little has been preserved through folklore has clearly been distorted and colored by later information. Only for the Inca period are there any materials of social organization upon which some reliance can be placed.

TABLE 5
CHRONOLOGY OF CULTURES DEVELOPED
IN PRE-HISPANIC PERU

COASTAL REGIONS	APPROXIMATE PERIOD	HIGHLAND REGIONS
Chavín and Paracas	? B.C.-A.D. 500	Chavín and unknown
Early Chimu and Nazca	A.D. 600-800	Recuay, early Tiahuanaco
Contact with highlands	A.D. 800-900	Contact with coast
Coast Tiahuanaco	A.D. 900-1200	Late Tiahuanaco
Period of decline	A.D. 1200-1300	Period of decline
Late Chimu, Chancay, late Nazca, Ica	A.D. 1300-1400	Rise of Inca
Inca	A.D. 1400-1530	Inca

Source: Chronology and classification derived from Means, pp. 48-49 and Bennett, p. 80.

THE LAND SYSTEM OF THE INCAS

The empire of the Incas rose, as must have those which preceded it, through a major tribal group conquering its neighbors. The motivation for such aggressions is not clear. Possibly they developed over territorial disputes, which led to raids and retaliation. Tribute was frequently exacted from the conquered tribes, but there is no evidence that the early Inca group sought to build up a domain for this reason.[11] Systematized exaction of tribute under the Incas, and the consequent development of their empire, probably did not begin until the fifteenth century. Wendell Bennett has maintained that even at this time the goal was the development of a well-integrated economy rather than the mere exploitation of conquered peoples.[12] If so, one must marvel at the aplomb of the Inca rulers in choosing this method of achieving economic welfare, but the results appear to have justified their self-confidence.

It was apparently the early practice of the Incas to extract from conquered tribes the annual produce of a designated portion of the *marca*. There was probably no great disturbance of the internal structure of the *ayllu,* and often the ruling *curacas* were left to serve as local authorities so long as they agreed to follow the orders of the Incas. At least in its earlier phases the Inca Empire was a rather loose confederation of tribal units bound together by the imposition of the bureaucratic superstructure of the ruling group. As they gained more experience as rulers, the Incas expanded not only through conquest but also through a program of colonization. The method of integrating a new area into the state became institutionalized, operating in the manner described by Padre Bernabé Cobo, one of the more reliable chroniclers:

The Inca, in settling a town or reducing it to his obedience, marked out its bounds and divided the fields and gardens in three parts in this manner: one part was assigned to the religion and cult of his false gods; another he took for himself; and the third remained for the community use of the said village. It could not be verified whether these parts in each village and province were equal, though it is clear that this division was not made in equal parts in many places but conformed in each territory to the density and quantity of the people thereof, . . . consideration always being given that the villages remain well provided with sustenance.[13]

This division of the cultivated lands into three parts is also described by Garcilaso de la Vega, who, though less reliable than Padre Cobo, antedates him. There is disagreement among the authorities as to whether the Incas became the owners of the conquered lands, granting usufruct to the subject peoples, or whether the *ayllus* remained in possession, merely paying the tribute demanded of them.[14] Jorge Basadre produces strong evidence in support of the former position, holding that the Incas had at least implicit dominion over the agricultural lands. This is inferred from the fact that the rulers exercised complete authority over woods and pasture lands and that, furthermore, they felt free to transfer entire tribes from one site to another.[15]

The produce from the lands of the Inca was used to provide for the food needs of governing functionaries, as well as for the general maintenance of the ruling class. The lands of the Sun, as those dedicated for religious purposes were called, were used not only to maintain the numerous priests and their retinues but also to furnish provisions for religious feasts and sacrifices. The lands retained for community use continued to be distributed among the family heads, as had been the practice prior to subjugation, the individual assignment being governed by the size of the family. Garcilaso, in a detailed discussion of the subject, asserts that a *tupu* of land was given to each married couple, with an extra *tupu* added to the family plot on the birth of each son and half a *tupu* for each daughter. The son retained his *tupu* on beginning a family of his own, but that of the daughter reverted to the community for redistribution upon her marriage.[16] Each family received the harvest from its own lands, but there were also community lands whose produce was in part distributed to the widowed, orphaned, aged, and infirm, and in part deposited in storehouses, called *pirwas*, for use in periods of poor harvest. The lands of the Inca and the Sun were worked in common by the members of the community on a draft basis, the system being called the *mita*. Mutual assistance was generally practiced in the cultivation and harvest of family plots.

There is some evidence indicating that a system of private property was developing under the Inca regime. Lands were frequently given by the Inca rulers to lesser officials whom they wished to favor. These donations generally carried with them a stipulation that they could not be transferred except through inheritance. It was also usually required that the heirs should possess the inheritance in common rather than divide it into individual lots.[17] This quasi-private property was worked by the individual owners without community aid, and it is highly possible that in cases of large areas some of the lands were rented to other community members. Another trend in the direction of a private property system was in the periodic assignment of community lands to family heads. Frequently this developed into a mere formality, as the same lands were assigned to the same families each year. In some instances it appeared that the rights to a particular family plot were hereditary, although not otherwise transferable.[18]

The main contribution of the Inca Empire was the social and cultural unification of numerous and diverse tribes spread over a wide

area. This was to be seen in the establishment of Quechua as a
national tongue (except among the stubborn Aymara) and the
standardization of local political organization. It was the peculiar
administrative genius of the Incas that made possible the construction
of elaborate public works such as the famed roads, bridges, and irrigation systems despite relatively crude tools and a heavy dependence
upon human energy. There seems little doubt, either, that the
authoritarian political system was responsible for an agricultural productivity which, despite the severe natural limitations, was able to
sustain a population of approximately five million. Yet, ironically, it
was also the rigidly structured political system which made possible
the incredibly easy conquest of the Incas by a few Spaniards under
the leadership of the venturesome Francisco Pizarro.

The Colonial Era

The story of the conquest of Peru is too familiar to recount here, but
it should be noted that the Spanish throne was relatively well prepared to
deal with this new addition to the royal dominion, at least in comparison
with some of the earlier acquisitions. Francisco Pizarro had formed
his expeditionary partnership with Diego de Almagro and Padre
Fernando de Luque in 1524, but it was not until some seven years later
that the actual conquest group left Panama for Peru. By that time
Spain had had four decades of experience in dealing with its New
World, sufficient enough time to frame a number of important policies.
In the earlier periods most policy making had been of an *ad hoc* nature,
expressed in the form of royal decrees. The Council of the Indies had
then been organized in the same year that Pizarro went into the aforementioned partnership. This council thenceforth served as an executive, legislative, and judicial body for the colonies. A separate organization, the *Casa de Contratación,* was established to handle trade and
travel to the Western Hemisphere.

Some evidence of the general land policy that had been formulated is to be seen in the royal *capitulaciones,* or contracts, accorded to
Pizarro in July of 1529 for the conquest of Peru. Most of the explora-
tions and conquests of the period, it is to be remembered, were of a

private-enterprise nature, with the conquistadors operating under such royal charters. Pizarro, who did the actual negotiating for the contracts, fared much better under their terms than did his two partners: he was appointed governor, captain-general, and *adelantado* of the territory of Peru.[19] The appointment to the position of *adelantado* was by far the most important of the three, being what the Spanish scholar José M. Ots Capdequí has called "the most outstanding title conceded to the chief of a discovery expedition."[20] It was a lifetime appointment, usually, and in some cases hereditary for two or more generations. The *adelantado* was conceded the right to allot lands, apportion Indians, and appoint public officials in the new territory, plus whatever additional privileges were granted in his specific charter.

The *capitulación* of Pizarro simply stated that he could use the office in the way in which it had been used in the rest of the Indies. Since there had been considerable variation in the uses to which the office had been put, Pizarro must have been perplexed as to what his rights and privileges were. At any rate, with a show of circumspection that was quite out of character, he sent one Sebastián Rodrígues to the Spanish court for a definite ruling on the matter, which was subsequently accorded in a royal decree of May 21, 1534, issued by Charles V. This decree supplied the solicited clarification:

. . . for the present [time] I give you full faculty to allot to the persons who are of the Conquest [expedition] and the present population of said province, as well as to those who go to live there in the future, town plots on which they can establish houses and gardens, and *peonías* and *caballerías* which they can work and sow, following the order and moderation that we have commanded to be followed in similar allotments, [and if] the citizens to whom you thus apportion them reside on them the five years which they are obliged to, we will make a grant of them and allow [the citizens] to own them just as the residents of our Indies own and may own the *caballerías* and [other] properties and houseplots that were allotted to them at our command and commission.[21]

It appears that the royal government was attempting to initiate a homestead policy in Peru at this early date, but from all indications grants of this type held little or no appeal for the conquistadors. These adventurers were far more interested in exploiting the rich mineral wealth which was known to exist in Peru. For such exploitation they needed manpower, and this could be obtained through concessions of jurisdictional rights over various segments of the Indian population, available under the *encomienda* system.

The system of *encomiendas,* which had originated during the reconquest of the Iberian Peninsula from the Moors, was transferred to the New World by Christopher Columbus.[22] It did not receive legal recognition, however, until the administration of Nícolas de Ovando in the West Indies during the early years of the sixteenth century. Despite a running battle to abolish the system, waged by various champions of Indian freedom, especially Padre Bartolomé de Las Casas, the *encomienda* was permitted in the new territory of Peru. In fact, as C. H. Haring has pointed out, the desire to attract settlers to the region may have been the primary factor in the return of the *encomienda* to public favor.[23] Francisco Pizarro, who was not a man to quibble over legal technicalities, despite his query about his royal charter, appears to have granted some *encomiendas* even before he received any authorization to do so.[24]

The *encomienda* was a political administrative unit as well as an economic unit, which meant that the grantee, or *encomendero,* was expected to fulfill certain functions and assume obligations as the crown's representative. Primarily, he was charged with seeing to the Christianization of the Indians under his charge and collecting royal tribute from them. While the *encomienda* carried with it certain administrative controls over the Indians of a given area, the grant did not give the *encomendero* any rights to the land itself.[25] It was the express intention of the crown that the Indians should retain possession of their lands and work them, but the *encomenderos* generally had other designs. As early as 1536 Charles V directed a special decree to Peru calling for ·a halt in the practice of removing Indians from agricultural lands of the *encomienda* territory for purposes of working in mines, which were often far removed. Failure to comply with the stipulations of the decree, it was warned, would be punished with the loss of the *encomienda* and a fine of ten thousand *maravedís.*[26]

There is no evidence that the *encomenderos* were greatly cowed by this order or similar ones issued from the distant Spanish court. Abuses of the *encomienda* continued in all parts of the empire until once again, this time with papal backing, the abolitionist group won the sympathy of Charles V. An investigation was made of the administration of the Council of the Indies, resulting in the promulgation of the New Laws of 1542-1543, which contained sweeping reforms.

The principal concern of the new legislation was the welfare of the Indians. The laws stipulated that the natives were free persons and subjects of the crown, and therefore should not be compelled to work against their will. All illegal *encomiendas* were to be returned to royal control, as were those of all religious orders and royal officials. No new *encomiendas* were to be awarded, and all existent legal *encomiendas* were to be returned to the crown upon the death of the incumbent *encomendero*. There were some special provisions in the laws pertaining to Peru, concerned for the most part with the bloody dispute that had arisen between Pizarro and Almagro over the jurisdictional rights in Cuzco. A number of *encomenderos* who had been involved in the dispute either lost their *encomiendas* or received lesser penalties. It seems apparent that the ultimate aim of the New Laws was the complete abolition of the *encomienda* system.

It was largely to enforce the stringent and unpopular regulations that a viceroy was appointed to Peru for the first time since the conquest. The hapless individual selected, one Blasco Nuñez Vela, proceeded to undertake his assigned task with considerably more zeal than tact. The combination of his mission and his attitude was sufficient to provoke a rebellion on the part of the disgruntled *encomenderos* led by Gonzalo Pizarro in 1544. The rebellion achieved temporary success in that Nuñez was assassinated and the New Laws were repealed in 1546.[27] The rebel group of Gonzalo Pizarro was in turn defeated, however, by a royal force under the leadership of Pedro de la Gasca. The *encomiendas* of the rebels were then confiscated and redistributed among the leaders of the counterrevolutionary forces, which left the basic system unaltered except for the change of personnel.[28]

Encomiendas continued to flourish in Peru for the remainder of the century, although some radical alterations were instituted by the viceroy Toledo, as will be noted shortly. By 1561, there were 427 private *encomienda* villages in Peru and 50 more that were unassigned.[29] Fifteen years later there were 695 *encomiendas,* involving nearly 400,000 tributary Indians. The system finally began to decline in the latter part of the seventeenth century, largely as a result of the demands of the financially burdened Hapsburgs for greater proportions of the tribute. In the years 1711, 1720, and 1721 a series of decrees was issued which placed all *encomiendas* under the administration of the crown as they became vacated through the deaths of the private holders.[30]

It will be remembered that Francisco Pizarro under his title of *adelantado* in Peru had the right to concede land grants as well as *encomiendas.* The two types of grants were separate, although an *encomendero* could also be, and undoubtedly generally was, a land grantee.[31] The first land grants appear to have been made in the town of San Miguel, founded by Pizarro in 1532. After the capture and execution of the Inca Emperor Atahualpa at Cajamarca in 1532, land grants and *encomiendas* were distributed in that region by Pizarro to his cohorts. Apparently he continued his generous distribution of land and Indians as his party journeyed southward, and after the completion of the conquest. By 1541, according to the seventeenth-century historian Fernando de Montesinos, the better lands had been distributed. In his *Anales del Perú—1498-1642* he wrote: "Although the land was vast, even by this time there was scarcely room for its inhabitants; there were some founders to whom 30 or 40 leagues appeared a small amount of land, and there were even some holdings of 50; and these included water, pastures, and royal roads."[32]

Such grants as those cited by Montesinos were directly contrary to royal instructions and were responsible for the issuance of the New Laws of 1542-1543 stipulating their reduction to a moderate size. Nevertheless, concentration of land in the hands of a few developed to such an extent that many of the Spanish newcomers were unable to get decent grants, and the Indian tribes were unable to retain their holdings. Numerous decrees and cedulas indicated the strong desire on the part of the Spanish rulers that the Indians should continue in possession of their agricultural lands, but such orders were not sufficient to restrain the encroachments of the Spanish subjects in the New World. Even those Indians who did not have their lands illegally appropriated were frequently unable to continue tillage because of their forced labor in the mines.

There were, of course, some Indian communities which were not assigned to private Spanish overlords; these continued to operate in much the same manner as they had under the Incas. The lands of the Inca and the Sun were usually divided among the villagers, but in many communities the practice of keeping the food storehouses filled with the produce of these fields was followed.[33] Theoretically, the Indian communities which had been assigned as *encomiendas* retained possession of their lands and, whenever possible, they too continued the traditions developed under the Incas.[34]

The year 1569 marked a new era in colonial policy with the appointment of the remarkable administrator Francisco de Toledo as fifth viceroy. With unprecedented zeal Toledo set about completely reorganizing the administrative system, being aided in his task by such legal savants as Polo de Ondegardo, Juan Matienze, Fernando de Santillán, and Sarmiento de Gamboa. Not content to direct his viceroyalty on the basis of the usual reports, from 1570 to 1576 the new executive conducted an extended personal tour which carried him to the farthest reaches of his assigned jurisdictional area. This tour apparently convinced him of the fact that a large number of *encomiendas* were not being run according to royal directions. With typical forthrightness, he therefore placed all the *encomenderos* directly under his own supervision and retracted the appointments of some of the worst offenders. Toledo also ordered all Indians who had not previously been assigned to some Spanish administrator placed in controlled villages (*reducciones*) because, in his own stern words, "it was not possible to indoctrinate such Indians without wresting them from their hiding places."[35]

The good or evil of Toledo's policies has been much debated, but champions and critics alike agree that they were sweeping in their scope and radical in their effects. The system of *reducciones* was conciously patterned after the organizational structure developed by the Incas and with more or less the same ends in view, in particular the exaction of tribute. If the legal precepts mirrored accurately the desires of the legislators, it might justly be said that the demands made upon the confined natives were really no more harsh than those imposed by the Inca administration. Unfortunately for the indigenous element, the reality was not so liberal as the theory. Torn from their *marcas,* which were frequently far distant from the *reducciones* to which they were sent, several *ayllus* would be assigned to the same village. Then, despite the decrees to the contrary, their vacated lands would be rapidly taken over by the Spanish. In all, some 614 *reducciones* were established during the Toledo regime.[36] Each of the *ayllus* assigned to a *reducción* was accorded a separate subdivision called a *parcialidad* or *comunidad.* Each *comunidad* possessed its own separate agricultural lands as well as residential quarter, and plots were distributed to the family heads in a manner quite similar to that which was traditional. The Indians continued to pay royal tribute and, in addition, were subject to a labor draft (which was called the *mita,* as had been the Inca equivalent) for work in the mines or weaving factories (*obrajes*). Under some of the more despotic local administrative officers the *mita* tended to develop into little more than a form of slavery. On the other hand, it should be pointed out that the *reducciones* provided land for some of the Indians who had previously been deprived of it, and some of the more fortunate communities actually prospered.[37]

Despite the hopes of the royal government, after several decades of Spanish occupation Peru failed to show signs of developing into a colony of prosperous, middle-class agriculturists. The reasons for this failure do not appear too complex. First, the early conquistadors were mostly adventurers and soldiers of fortune who had little interest in settling down on farms. Second, farmers of the type the crown encouraged as colonists had little status in Spain, and those who migrated to the New World for purposes of gaining status were not likely to choose small farming as an occupation. Third, the existence of mineral wealth in great quantities in Peru continually held out the promise of a quick fortune through mining, while small-scale agriculture held no such lure. Finally, the only type of agricultural enterprise that did carry with it prestige, the large estate operated with what was virtually slave labor, by its very nature precluded the coexistence of any great numbers of more modest farms, if there were many of the plantation type.

Undismayed by these handicaps, the crown persisted in its efforts to encourage permanent settlers with such inducements as those offered by the New Discovery and Settlement Ordinances issued by Philip II in 1573. These ordinances continued the general homestead policy expressed in previous royal cedulas and offered generous land grants to those who would agree to establish Spanish colonial villages. Organizers of colonization projects were offered even greater rewards. The general specifications of the ordinances were that the colonial settlements should be villages of the Spanish type with a minimum of thirty settlers, who would be provided with specified numbers of farm animals of various types. It was also required that each new village should have a church and priest. The amount of land to be allotted for each village was four square leagues, but it was required that the new community be at least five leagues from any previous Spanish settlement and located so that it would not encroach on any other community, white or Indian, or any private holdings.³⁸ Each colonist in such a village was offered a house lot (*solar*) within the village, and farmlands on its outskirts. Pasture lands (*dehesas*) were to be the property of the village and used in common by all settlers. Other portions of the land, the *ejidos,* were to be set aside for distribution to future residents as the village expanded. A third form of village property, the *propios,* was to be retained by the municipality and rented to pay public expenses. All colonists were required to reside in the villages for a period of five years in order to secure full title to the lands.

The *poblador* who contracted with the royal government to establish a village was to be conceded a fourth of the total grant remaining after the deduction of *ejidos, propios,* and *dehesas.* If he failed to fulfill his contract, however, he not only forfeited his grant, plus whatever improvements he had made on it, but also had to pay a sizable fine.[39] The possible gains were probably well worth the risk, though. Since the total area of the village amounted to nearly 7,200 hectares, or approximately twenty-eight square miles, a successful organizer would have been provided with a comfortable estate of three or four thousand acres at the least. As an extra incentive he was allowed to entail his estate, which made it possible for him to pass it on intact to his heirs.

A constant cause of worry to the royal government was the practice of many, if not most, individuals who had received land grants of expanding their holdings far beyond their legal boundaries. In an attempt to stop this, the throne issued a cedula in 1591 ordering all lands which were held without just title to be returned immediately to the crown's domain.[40] When this order, like most similar to it, was generally ignored, another was promulgated in 1631. But the new order contained a significant passage which read as follows:

Considering it to the greater benefit of our vassals, we order and command the viceroys and governing officials to leave unchanged those lands [whose titles have been] adjusted by their predecessors, leaving their owners in peaceful possession; and to permit and issue new titles to those who have inserted and usurped more than the surveys show belongs to them upon [payment of] a moderate composition for the excess.[41]

The probable motives for the issuance of this order were to give better organization to the defective system of land titles on the one hand, and to bring in new fees to the royal treasury on the other. In practice it amounted to little more than the legalization of many completely fraudulent claims. As usual, the main victims of the legislation were the Indians, particularly those in the reducciones, who saw the lands they had been forced to vacate pass into the hands of Spaniards who paid the "moderate composition" to gain title. Later decrees in 1642 and 1646 attempted to remedy this situation by declaring inadmissible to composition any lands which had been taken from the Indians or which had not been in possession of the applicants for at least ten years.[42] By that time much of the Indian territory had already been lost. The losses were offset to some extent by the fact that the

Indians themselves could, and did, obtain legal titles to land under the same act. The few fortunate Indians who did thus acquire private land were then protected from swindles by an ordinance of the Toledo administration which prevented their disposing of their lands without special government permission.

A summary of the land legislation of the greater part of the seventeenth century is to be found in Title XII, Book IV, of the *Recopilación de las Leyes de los Reynos de las Indias*. Little new or noteworthy was added during the eighteenth century until the issuance of the Royal Instruction of 1754. This instruction provided that the viceroys and presidents of the royal *audiencias* should delegate special officers attached to the royal treasury to make all future sales and compositions of lands. It provided for the restoration of lands that had been fraudulently seized from Indian communities, but allowed composition of any lands whose titles had been obtained after 1700 without royal confirmation. Moreover, owners were allowed to gain title to, and confirmation of, lands which exceeded the bounds of their certified holdings. All other lands occupied without title were to be considered royal patrimonies and as such to be sold by the representatives of the crown.[43] The purposes of the instruction of 1754 were more or less the same as those of the Royal Cedula of 1631, but with greater emphasis on filling the depleted vaults of the royal treasury.[44] Like the earlier measure, that of 1754 was aimed at revising the land title system, but it did relatively little about the equally pressing problem of land distribution, except possibly to worsen it. Again the usurped holdings were brought into the legal hold, and again the Indians were offered paper protection against extortions which were considerably more tangible.

Concentration of ownership was characteristic of the Peruvian land system from the inception of the colonial era, despite the various legal measures directed at the prevention of latifundia. A considerable quantity of better lands was held by ecclesiastical organizations—churches, monasteries, convents, hospitals, schools, and charitable organizations—since it was customary practice to give generous grants to religious bodies upon the foundation of any new village. Other lands were probably acquired through purchase, although as early as 1535 a decree had been issued prohibiting the sale of private land grants to ecclesiastical institutions.[45] Many of the properties that passed into mortmain were endowments or bequests of faithful parishioners. The zealous influence of the clergy in securing such bequests is apparent from a decree issued in 1754 forbidding clerical interference in the preparation of wills.[46] Further inroads on available lands, chiefly agricultural, were made by various monastic orders serving as bankers during the colonial period; as such they were in a position to foreclose mortgages.[47] The chief drawback of ecclesiastical ownership was that once lands passed into the "dead hands" of the church they were no longer available for private circulation. Only with state seizure of the tremendous and widespread holdings of the Jesuit order (Society of Jesus) upon its expulsion in 1767 did private citizens again gain access to the ownership of such temporalities.[48]

It was primarily in the system of private holdings that the trend toward concentration of ownership was most clearly detected. The patterns and values of feudalism were transferred to the New World without significant alteration, the natives assuming the positions of serfs. Possession of good lands in quantity bestowed a unique prestige, which in turn furthered their acquisition. Once accumulated, large estates could be preserved intact through the practice of entailment (*mayorazgo*). Because land was considered more in terms of its symbolic than its utilitarian value, absentee ownership was widely practiced, not only in Peru but throughout Spanish America. The Spanish never showed any great inclination to leave the coastal cities of Peru for the hinterland, not only because of the greater accessibility of the coast but also, as Javier Prado has pointed out, because they were really urbanites at heart.[49] They wanted plantations, but they did not want to farm. They acquired magnificent farms and haciendas in various regions, but left them to the care of mestizo *mayordomos*. The owners were usually content to visit them only at planting and harvest seasons, or to spend brief periods of recreation or diversion. Even where the Spanish had introduced sugar cane, olives, rice, and grapes—for which the rich coastal valleys were ideally suited—they generally left the Negro slaves or Indian laborers to their own primitive devices so far as the actual cultivation was concerned. As a result, the yields were generally poor, but not sufficiently poor to alter the general practice.

The Indian land system during the colonial period deserves special consideration because it was that which underwent radical alterations under the impact of white settlement. There is every evidence that the Spanish throne was genuinely concerned about the welfare of the Indians, but there was a considerable divergence between the stated policy and the actual administration. Bustamante Cisneros called attention to this fact in his treatise on the Indian communities of Peru when he wrote:

On the one hand, there was an apparent system, purely ideological and formalistic, an artificial system that worked on paper and was translated into laws, provisions, ordinances, and royal decrees; on the other hand, there was developing a real, or sociological, system resulting from the interaction of the actual factors of the milieu, a live system in the realm of reality, which had the consecration of facts and which reflected not the generous idealism of the Spanish monarchs but the mean interests of the conquerors.[50]

The effect of the "mean interests" upon the Indian population is seen in the tremendous numerical losses suffered by them during the colonial period. The exact extent of this loss is difficult to estimate because no records of the preconquest population are available, although the Incas maintained highly accurate enumerations of this nature. The better estimates of the population under Inca domination range from four-and-a-half million to around seven million,[51] yet in the first colonial census, conducted under the administration of the viceroy Gil de Taboada in 1791, the total population including whites and Indians was only slightly over a million.[52] Some of this prodigious decrease has been attributed to the migration of native peoples from the territory of the viceroyalty.[53] However, it is well known that the natives fell victim by the thousands to epidemics introduced by the Spanish. The close contact necessitated through confinement in the *reducciones* and mass labor in the mines and *obrajes* provided ideal conditions for the spread of contagious diseases. One medical expert has expressed the opinion that smallpox alone could have accounted for the demographic disaster during the period, but other diseases also contributed to the net result. Chief among them were probably measles and scarlet fever, which were new to the country and were especially lethal among the infantile population.[54]

Contemporary reports also testify to the unhappy condition of the Indians. Among those considered most reliable are the accounts of the royal emissaries Jorge Juan and Antonio de Ulloa, who conducted an official investigation of the conditions in Peru between 1735 and 1745. From their observations at the time, they wrote:

One of the things that most move one to compassion for those people, the Indians, is to see them now totally dispossessed of their lands, for although at the beginning of the Conquest and upon the establishment of their villages they were assigned allotments to be divided among the resident Indians and their *caciques,* the omnipresent cupidity has operated to such an extent that at present the holdings remaining to them are greatly reduced, and most are without any. Some were deprived of their lands by having them forcibly taken from them; others because the owners of neighboring haciendas exerted so much pressure that they sold them for whatever price was offered; and others because they were tricked into relinquishing them.[55]

Within the *reducciones* themselves, the royal investigators further noted, there was considerable exploitation of the Indians by both Spanish and Indian administrative officers, as well as by the priests. Juan and Ulloa commented also upon the tendency of both village and farm properties to accumulate in the hands of the churches and various religious orders.[56] Even allowing for possible exaggerations, the conditions depicted by Juan and Ulloa, as well as by other contemporary observers, are almost directly antithetical to those which the Spanish legislators had hoped to create.

The wrecking of the Inca system created social and economic crises for the Indians that were resolved in a variety of different ways. As already mentioned, many fell victim to disease, overwork, and probably starvation brought on by the disruption of agricultural activities. Others fled southward and eastward. Thousands were placed in controlled villages where their welfare was largely dependent upon the type of administrator to whom they were encharged. The remainder probably stayed where they were, on lands which had become part of a private hacienda. The lot of those who "stayed put" was also largely dependent upon the character of the owners, but the known fact that many Indians fled the *reducciones* to live as gratuitous laborers, or *yanaconas,* suggests that the conditions of the private haciendas were in many instances less arduous. At any rate, the latter offered freedom from the numerous extortions and oppressions of petty civil and clerical officials, and frequently the opportunity to continue in the tradition of *ayllu* life.

In summarizing the man-land relational aspects of the colonial era, it may be said that the impact of Spanish culture upon the system obviously produced major changes, among them the complete upsetting, though by no means the obliteration, of the Inca pattern. Of fundamental significance was the introduction on a wide scale of the concept of private property, a feature which was rare, although not unknown, under the Inca regime. All the land of the Inca Empire was claimed for the Spanish monarchy by right of conquest and made available to private individuals through grants issued by the crown's representatives. In theory, the Indians, as royal subjects, had the same right to acquire land as did the whites, but in practice most of the grants were awarded to Spaniards. One can easily understand how bewildering the bureaucratic procedure and title system must have been to the ordinary natives. Lacking familiarity with the operations of the private property system, they fell easy victims to the chicaneries of avaricious whites who took every advantage of their ignorance.

Even though privately owned property became the accepted form, communal ownership was not abolished by the Spanish. The *reducciones* instituted by the viceroy Toledo utilized a system of landed property which was patterned directly after the Inca system, as has been previously noted. In addition, the *dehesas,* or village pasture lands, were used in common and were typical features of Spanish villages. The *ejidos* and *propios* were more properly municipal lands, but were still distinct from private holdings.

Concentration of ownership was certainly one of the more significant developments of the colonial period and operated to the detriment of the colonists as much as of the natives. At least, the latter were able to subsist by living as unpaid laborers on the large estates, a course which was not open to the proud Castilians. Ironically, the landless Spaniards frequently fell to the care of charitable orders, who justified their own extensive landholdings on the grounds that so many poverty-stricken people were dependent upon their mercy. While the colonial government tried to protect Indian lands on the one hand, on the other it tacitly condoned their theft by giving legal title to fraudulent extensions of grants upon the payment of the composition fee. Large estates, once accumulated, tended to remain intact or grow larger because of the prestige incentive for the amassing of landed wealth, because there was a plentiful supply of cheap labor with which to maintain them, and because of the law under which they could be entailed.

THE NINETEENTH-CENTURY REPUBLIC

Peru was not one of the centers of rebellion against royal dominion that sprang up during the early nineteenth century. On the contrary, it remained loyal to crown interests long after other sections of the far-flung empire had declared their independence. Furthermore, the liberal theme which typified some elements of the revolutionary movement was almost totally absent in Peru after it once became involved. If any rebellious thought prevailed, it was in reactionary views held by the more conservative elements who hoped to abate the liberal colonial legislation which had hindered, if not prevented, the enlargement of their own personal acquisitions. On this point, Romero has written: "In reality, the revolution for independence was lacking in agrarian content. The three hundred proprietor families on the coast continued during the Independence and upon the establishment of the Republic as the class dominating the land, together with the Church and its extensive properties."[57] There is little evidence that the founding of the Republic of Peru signified a true social revolution. Aspirations for social reforms were high, but few were realized. Setting a pattern for the revolutions to follow, the struggle for independence had as its main effect a change in political administration.

However lacking Peru may have been in native liberalism at the time of independence, the reform ideals of the French Revolution of three decades before were clearly evident in the legislation sponsored in Peru by San Martín, Bolívar, and their adherents. Of particular interest were their ideas concerning the land system and the status of the Indian population—ideas which when converted into legislation had significant effects, but not the intended ones.

While the War of Emancipation was yet in progress, San Martín in his role as Protector of the Liberty of Peru issued several decrees, in August of 1821, proclaiming the Indians to be full citizens of the new Republic. The decrees specifically abolished personal tribute and involuntary servitude of the autochthonous group.[58] With Bolívar's rise to dictatorship of the country in 1823, several more decrees were issued with the intention of converting the Indians into small landowners and of abolishing the system of *reducciones*. The first of these decrees, published in April of 1824, ordered that all state lands with the exception of those occupied by the Indian population be offered for sale. The lands of the *reducciones* were to be distributed among the occupants, who were to be entitled to full legal ownership of their apportionments. Preference was to be given to those who were already located on the sites, but it was specified that no Indian should remain without a share of the land.[59]

Bolívar's intent, in keeping with the new liberal thought of the period, was to establish a democratic nation of small, independent farmers. It seems obvious from these legal prescriptions, though, that he was completely lacking in an understanding of the reality and complexity of the situation with which he was attempting to deal. His own bitter realization of the fiasco of his initial attempt to carry out his philosophy is apparent in a decree of July 4, 1825. In its prologue, the Liberator noted that, despite the earlier law, the distribution of lands had not been carried out in just proportion, that most of the natives still did not have the use or possession of their lands, and that a great portion of the lands had been usurped by the various authorities who had been charged with their distribution. He therefore ordered that the lands be apportioned in accordance with the earlier order, including those lands that had been illegally appropriated. The decree stated explicitly that each Indian "regardless of age and sex shall receive a *topo* of land in the fertile and irrigated places . . . [and] two *topos* in the sterile and unirrigated places." To thwart future embezzlements, a provision was included that those Indians who received lands could not dispose of them before the year 1850, and never to ecclesiastical bodies, under penalty of nullification of the grant.[60]

The difficulties of executing these orders may be deduced from the revealing circulars dispatched by the presidents of the governing councils, especially of the Minister of the Treasury, De Pando. The latter officially noted, in a circular sent to departmental prefects in 1826, that Bolívar's decrees had still not been followed. This was followed by another circular, dispatched in February of 1827, in which De Pando ordered the officials who were distributing the lands to refrain from exceeding their commissions in such ways as issuing unauthorized titles for illegal fees.[61] Finally the Constituent Congress ordered the complete suspension of sales and distribution of the state lands until an investigation could be made of the activities and progress of the various land commissions. In the following year, 1828, a new General Constituent Congress sought to clear up the situation by promulgating a new decree which ordered lands to be distributed to those who had not yet received any. The decree reaffirmed the stand that Indians and mestizos were legal owners of their lands, with the exception that the right of disposal was allowed only to those who were literate.[62]

The new Constitution of 1828 contributed to the formulation of a national land policy in prohibiting the entailment of estates and declaring the right of religious bodies to dispose freely of their holdings. It is doubtful that the latter clause had any great effect, since the restraining influence on the disposition of church lands had never been secular law, but perhaps the legislators hoped thus to pry lands loose from the "dead hands." As had been the case with most of the colonial legislation, the regulations of the republican government were apparently violated as much as they were followed. Exploitation of the Indians continued, not only at the hands of the whites but also, by this time, at the hands of their own leaders, or *caciques,* who were generally of mixed blood. This social betrayal manifested an extreme state of disorganization among the Indians, which the Peruvian jurist José Frisancho has attributed directly to the land policy of the early republic. He writes:

The adventitious legislation of the Republic changed the form of agrarian property of the Indians in Peru abruptly, modifying it into a premature and disintegrating individualism conducive to *caciquismo.* . . . From the moment the prohibition of the Indian to sell his lands was lifted, his position was indefensible against the advances of the land-grabbers; these latter, being incomparably stronger and more skilled in artifice, through grouping themselves in coalitions for their mutual advantage were able to dislodge the small Indian landowners from their holdings without any great difficulty.[63]

The well-intended but ill-administered liberal land policy of the early years of the republic soon became hopelessly obscured in the political struggles of a whole series of *caudillos,* those self-appointed governors, usually military men, who sought to run the nation. The energies of such men were almost entirely directed toward either rising to power or maintaining themselves once they had achieved control. During the years of fruitless and bloody attempts to unite Peru and Bolivia, internal legislation was all but forgotten. The havoc wrought by six military campaigns in the cause of unity over a period of fourteen years would probably have been sufficient to forestall the application of any policies even had they been formulated. But agrarian and land problems seemed absent from the minds of the political leaders. "The countryside, apart from its landscape value, roads, springs, and scenery, was far from the political struggle," Basadre has noted. "In Peru there did not appear an ideology like that of Rivadavía that planned a new distribution of the land. Agrarian factions were missing in the civil wars. . . ."[64]

Not until the rise of the mestizo *caudillo* Ramón Castilla to the presidency of the republic in 1864 was there sufficient stability to permit any sort of sustained legislation. During his first elected term, from 1845 to 1851, a law was passed abolishing existing entailments, indicating that the article of the 1828 Constitution dealing with entailments had not been effectual. The first Peruvian civil code was also formulated under Castilla, but it was not put into effect until 1852 under the Echenique administration. The code of 1852 picked up the broken threads of liberalism that had run through the 1820's and defined the status of the Indian as simply a Peruvian citizen with the same legal rights as whites and mestizos. The legislators who devised the code either assumed or hoped that the Indians had become accustomed to the system of private land ownership, but subsequent developments proved to the contrary. As had been the case with almost all previous liberal legislation, the letter of the law was twisted by the clever and unscrupulous to serve ends directly contrary to those that had been intended. To quote Emilio Romero on the subject:

History demonstrates, in fact, that it was immediately following the promulgation of the old Civil Code of 1852 that the latifundian oligarchies began to be formed in Peru. . . . And history shows also that shortly after the Code was promulgated the laws of judicial and civil proceedings were promulgated, fatal instruments through which, using a Roman institution, the interdict, Indians even until the present day have been made the easy prey of the large landholders, and not only the Indians, but also the *cholos* and mestizos.[65]

It would be a gross oversimplification to attribute the growth of large holdings during the republic primarily to the Civil Code of 1852 and the associated procedural rules mentioned by Romero. It is doubtful that any legal forms could have prevailed against the organized opposition of the economically powerful, who were guided and sustained by both tradition and ambition.

Aside from its social consequences, the code of 1852 is a convenient bench mark for the onset of a new phase of economic development in Peru. Beginning with the Castilla administration, the nation set forth on a program of industrial and commercial expansion based largely upon exports of guano, the rich fertilizer obtained from the desert islands off the coast. The natural nitrates of the southern deserts were also popular on European markets, and the ease of extraction made profits high. The flush times were soon symbolized in the undertaking of a vast program of public works, particularly national railroads along the coast and joining the coast to the sierra. For the first time since the founding of the republic coastal agriculture began to flourish. Previously it had been in a depressed state as a result of the constant civil turmoil which had not only seen frequent crop destruction by invading armies but also caused a severe labor shortage, since many farm laborers were recruited in support of one cause or another. The abolition of slavery in 1855 had eliminated that labor source and further aggravated the problem. Equally serious, and also traceable to the civil wars, was the lack of investment capital necessary for commercial agriculture.[66] Hence, the fresh flow of money into Peru marked the end of a long economic drought. Happily for the coastal farmers, it came at a time when European markets were desperately searching for new sources of cotton, the supply from the United States having been severely curtailed by the War Between the States.

Despite its auspicious beginnings the wave of economic prosperity soon broke upon unforeseen reefs; and the trough of depression that followed was long and deep. While numerous factors contributed to the national bankruptcy that came in the latter part of the nineteenth century, the major contribution to the general disaster was the war with Chile from 1879 to 1883. Fundamentally, the war was an economic struggle over the rich nitrate fields of the Atacama and Tarapacá deserts. The boundaries of those territories were unsettled and considered of no real importance until the value of the nitrate deposits contained in them was realized. Ironically, the boundary disputes were largely between Chile and Bolivia, but Peru became quickly and disastrously embroiled. Just as a chain of fortunate events had produced prosperity, a series of related calamities spiraled the economy downward into utter ruin. First, the national economic surplus was quickly drawn off by the cost of waging the war. Then, with the loss of the war to Chile, Peru was forced to cede its own nitrate fields of Tarapacá. Finally, as Chile's nitrate exports increased, the price of guano on the world market dropped to a fraction of what it had previously been. As the foreign-held bonds which had supported the ambitious, over-expanded, and to some extent corrupt, public works program came due, they were defaulted. Adding to the crisis was the revelation that much of the currency which had been issued by the numerous banks of Lima was completely without backing. The collapse was complete. For a decade a real system of national finance was utterly lacking. Finally, with the fiscal reforms instituted by the Piérola administration (1895-1899), the nation began to show signs of an economic resurrection.

THE TWENTIETH CENTURY

The dawn of the twentieth century in Peru witnessed the slow resumption of the industrialization process which had been halted by the succession of war, depressions, and finally internal political strife. Commercial agriculture, which had briefly flourished during the nitrate and guano boom, showed the same ill effects as other business enterprises. Its condition at the time has been described by the Peruvian agricultural authority Gerardo Klinge as follows:

At the beginning of the twentieth century, the agriculture of the coast was in a pitiful state. The area under cultivation, which had never equaled the area irrigated, had been curtailed as a consequence of the War of 1879 and the revolutions that followed, which disorganized production, destroyed working resources, and deprived agriculturists of even the most necessary work stock. The only agricultural export product worthy of mention was sugar. A little cotton was also exported, and small quantities of select-grade rice, but the imports of Asiatic rice exceeded the exports. The greater part of the cultivated lands was dedicated to subsistence crops to take care of a population smaller than the present one, with a very low level of living. Furthermore, agriculture was of a markedly extensive character, and the art of farming extremely backward.[67]

The effects of economic depression were not so noticeable in the sierra, as conditions there had changed little since the colonial period. Of passing interest, though, is the fact that the selva experienced a brief rubber boom in the latter part of the nineteenth century, that continued on into the twentieth, so that area was probably better off economically than before. The production of latex was purely on an extraction basis; no major attempts were made to establish domestic plantations.

Part of the economic restabilization program of Peru involved the control of basic transportation and productive industries by the foreign bondholders who had suffered such heavy financial losses as a result of national insolvency. These disputed concessions undoubtedly encouraged investments of more foreign capital, no small part of which went into coastal agriculture. National capital, as well, was increasingly invested in commercial agricultural enterprises devoted almost exclusively to the production of sugar cane and cotton. Significantly, two of the new type of sugar *hacendados,* Manuel Prado and Augusto Leguía, served as Peruvian presidents for twenty of the first thirty years of the twentieth century.

The relationship between political administration and industrialization during the first half of the twentieth century was largely a matter of attitudes toward foreign investors. When the inclination was favorable, the process speeded up; but even under the least receptive administrations there was no complete interruption of the transformation. For that matter, the differences in attitudes were not primarily concerned with whether industrialization should take place. It was a question of whether it should take place under national or foreign auspices. But since Peru was not technologically equipped to develop industry, the question was not realistic when first raised and perhaps still is not realistic today. Practically, a decision against foreign capital was a decision against industry, a fact well known to all those concerned with the issue, whatever their stand. The matter was one that seldom found loud expression in political campaigns, yet it was a significant consideration in the determination of the tenure and strength of any government in power.

It must be noted that Peru, like many other Latin American countries, has never been able to establish a tradition of elected national leadership. Elections have been held, of course, and men placed in presidential office as a consequence. Nevertheless, the democratically elected president is a much less typical figure than the *caudillo* who has forcibly seized national control. The pattern of succession by seizure began almost immediately after the founding of the "republic" and has not yet abated. Hence, the economic and military support which a presidential aspirant could muster has frequently been of greater importance than his popularity with the voters. Rarely, in recent times, have the military and economic forces been in different camps.

For an understanding of political and economic forces in recent decades, the national administrations may be briefly reviewed. One of the most enigmatic political personalities of the early part of the century was Augusto Leguía. Leguía served an elected presidential term from 1908 through 1912, returning to national leadership after a coup d'état in 1919. He remained as dictator for eleven years. The difficulty in understanding Leguía lies in the complete lack of consistency between his expressed political philosophy and his actual rule. As a political philosopher, he is to be ranked among the leading liberals of the day; as an administrator, he was arbitrary and conservative. One of the first acts of his second administration was to promulgate the Constitution of 1920, a model for republican government. There is no evidence that he ever felt any compulsion to follow its provisions. Parenthetically, one of the radical innovations contained in this Constitution was with regard to the Indians and their lands. The Indian communities were finally accorded official recognition as legal entities after nearly a century of legislation aimed at converting the community members into individual property holders.

Leguía's long tenure may possibly be explained in part by the fact that his impetuous legislation continually offered hope to liberal and conservative elements alike, although he was not completely acceptable to either. The only logic that can be detected in the contradictory themes was that of keeping himself in power. Throughout his administration the most liberal measures of their time were written into law, only to be nullified by peremptory acts of a completely overbearing nature.

Leguía had a genius for attracting foreign capital, which supported an ambitious public works program that included highways and irrigation projects. Some of the money undoubtedly found its way into the private coffers of those who were in favor with the administration, while critics of the president's methods were likely to find themselves summarily imprisoned or deported. This ability to attract foreign investments was undoubtedly responsible for his longevity in office, and when they ceased as a result of the international depression of the 1930's Leguía fell from power. He died in prison in 1932.

Leguía's successor was another *caudillo,* but of a cruder sort— Sánchez Cerro. As leader of the revolution which overthrew Leguía, Sánchez called for general elections and offered himself as the presidential candidate. His military control was a powerful campaign weapon, sufficient to "elect" him president despite the fact that the left-wing Aprista candidate Victor Raúl Haya de la Torre was more popular.[68] Except for the formulation of a new constitution, little of a constructive nature was accomplished under the new president before he was assassinated, to no one's surprise, in 1933. A constituent congress thereupon elected Oscar Benavides to serve in the presidential office during the critical period. Amidst incessant political turmoil general elections were called in 1936. However, when it appeared that the Aprista candidate Luis A. Eguiguren had won, Benavides declared the elections void and remained as dictator until 1939. During his administration he promulgated the Civil Code of 1936, which like the constitutions of 1920 and 1933 accorded full recognition to the Indian communities as legal entities.

In 1939 elections were again held, and the conservative Manuel Prado succeeded to the presidency. He served a full term of six years. His administration was marked by a program of public works made possible largely through the increased national prosperity brought on by World War II. Prado's successor, Bustamante, was somewhat more susceptible to left-wing influence, and, as a consequence, served but half of his elected term before being overthrown in a bloodless coup that once more placed national leadership in the hands of the familiar military *caudillo.* The new self-appointed executive, General Manuel A. Odría, presided over a military junta for two years before calling for elections in 1950. The presidential office was won handily by General Odría himself, after the only opposition candidate was imprisoned. Odría's policies have generally been highly favorable to the stimulation of foreign capital investment.

In reviewing the dozen decades of Peruvian political independence, it would appear that alterations of the social and economic systems were effected less by legislation directed toward this end than by the spontaneous interplay of other factors. This observation would seem to apply in particular to the system of man-land relations. The effects of the War of Independence upon the agrarian system, for example, were not so radical as might have been expected. It is true that San Martín and Bolívar, under the influence of eighteenth-century liberalism, sought to develop a social and economic structure based upon small landholders. But their lack of judgment concerning the prevailing moral and social climate was clearly evidenced by the widespread practices of graft and extortion which developed when the earnest attempt to distribute state lands to the Indians was made. The complete futility of seeking to implement their policy was obscured by the series of civil wars, which offered a rational excuse for the obvious ineffectuality. Thus the philosophic ideal that the Indians should be on an equal social and economic footing with the whites continued to find expression in legislation, though not in actual practice, for the remainder of the century.

Economic developments which were to alter substantially the agriculture of the coast were apparent in the latter half of the nineteenth century as cotton and sugar plantations enjoyed a brief prosperity based on fertilizer exports. The war with Chile and the subsequent internal strife plunged the nation into a depression which again reduced coastal agriculture to a bare subsistence level. With the re-establishment of a relative stability in the political and economic spheres, coastal agriculture experienced a new upsurge as foreign capital, as well as domestic, was invested in the commercial production of sugar cane and cotton. The hacienda gave way to the corporation farm on the coast, but still retained its dominance in the sierra, where it competed with the Indian communities for arable land. The latter had finally been recognized as legal entities, but perhaps too late for their own preservation. At any rate, the contrast and conflict of the disparate agricultural systems produced in the twentieth century a complexity of man-land relational problems that are encountered at every turn of the economy.

3.

Current Patterns of Land Distribution

LAND DISTRIBUTION is one of those emotionally charged subjects that tempt even those who should know better to make dogmatic assertions and unwarranted generalizations. It is commonplace to point out the social ills that accompany concentration of land ownership, and without too much effort one can cite a dozen instances of revolutions or near-revolutions with "land reform" as their theme. There is no intention here of entering into a discussion as to whether land distribution does play an important role in social and economic welfare; that is assumed. What is offered is a view that the effect of a particular pattern of land distribution lies not in the pattern itself but in its relationships with a number of other variables—social, cultural, and natural environmental.

Before pursuing this subject further, it would be well to clarify what is meant here by "land distribution." In ordinary usage the term refers to two different, but related, matters. One is the distribution of tenure statuses, in particular the status of owner. The other is the division of the land into separate holdings of various sizes. The stating of relationships between the size of holdings and the distribution of ownership status is a type of temptation to which reference was made in the first paragraph in this chapter. One is tempted to say, "Where much of the land area is in a relatively small number of large holdings, only a few individuals will be landowners." Peru offers quick exception; more than half a million Peruvians were classified as owners or landlords of agricultural lands in the 1940 Census, but tens of thousands of these owned less than an acre apiece. There is also the temptation to say, "When much of the land is owned by a small proportion of the population, a pattern of large holdings can be expected." Again, instances can be pointed out in Peru, as well as in a number of other places in the world, where owners of large plantations have subdivided their land into medium or small units which are leased to separate tenants or sharecroppers.

If the relating of ownership and size of holdings offers logical hazards, the assertion of glib generalizations about the effects of land distribution upon social functioning is an academic exercise fraught with pitfalls. Yet the dangers deter few. They can always make sweeping reference to the "lessons of history," whatever they may be, to substantiate their arguments. As earlier stated, this view assumes that the same type of distribution will produce the same consequences regardless of the other factors involved. Usually the view, still in keeping with eighteenth-century liberalism, is that the most satisfactory distribution is one of moderate-sized holdings for all, while the least satisfactory distribution is one of concentrated ownership and large holdings. This may be true, but it is not self-evident. Furthermore, it carries with it an implicit value judgment as to what is "satisfactory" which many persons and peoples will find unacceptable. This assumption of a universal standard was a mistake made by the Spanish royal government in its legislation pertaining to the Indians, a mistake which was carried on into the nineteenth century by the leaders of the independence movement.

Looking again, for the moment, at the Inca system of man-land relations, it is seen that the distribution of status and land was controlled either by the state or by the local community. In theory, the land was owned by the state and assigned to the community. The community assigned plots to family heads, the size of the plot being governed by the size of the family and the quality of the land. There was no competition for land, except perhaps in the case of some choice plot that had been vacated by the death of some family head. But even under this system the tradition developed of awarding the rights of tillage to one of the male lineal descendants. Individual initiative was necessary to produce a good yield, but in cultivation the principle of cooperation through labor exchange seems to have prevailed over competitiveness. Incentives were provided by the dependence of each family upon the harvest of its own land for its subsistence and by the punishment accorded lazy individuals. There was no great opportunity for individual advancement, at least for the ordinary subject. To the Western mind molded in the tradition of free enterprise, political independence, profit incentives, and aspirations to high status, the Inca system seems authoritarian and oppressive. Doubtless, to the Indian mind the Spanish system seemed equally undesirable. Not only did the Inca subjects fail to appreciate the superiority of a system of individual ownership, but they continued in their own system even when they were given the privilege of being "free" subjects of the Spanish monarch. In fact, some communities persisted in their traditional practices even after they were "liberated" a second time by the founders of the Republic of Peru.

Had the theory and the practice of Spanish colonial policy coincided more closely, it is possible that the Indians might have appreciated more the philosophy of individual ownership. It has already been established that the crown encouraged the distribution of land in moderate quantities to all who desired it. It has also been established that the royal government was unable to enforce its policy in the New World. The attitude of the Spanish conquerors and colonists is not difficult to understand, even though one may not sympathize with it. Their social system was one that rewarded material acquisition with prestige. Landed property was an ideal acquisition because it provided functional as well as symbolic wealth. A man with enough land under cultivation, even with poor yields, could derive enough income to live well in the city where the "man-of-property" symbol was appreciated. And lands were easily acquired, at least by the early comers, simply through wresting them from the Indians. The colonial legislation made such acquisition easy for a shrewd man, while the administration of the laws made it easy even for a stupid one. The real pinch came when most of the better lands had been taken over by the whites. Late-comers either were left landless or had to go so far to get land that it was hardly worth the effort.

Another function which landed property could serve was that of a rental source. This accounted for the acquisition of such large quantities of land by churches and organized charities, although some of the monastic orders actually worked their own lands. The major effect of the accumulation of lands by such organizations was to make it increasingly difficult for individuals to gain ownership rights to lands that were easily accessible. And even though a man might have gained a good income from cultivation of rented lands, the prestige factor of being a landowner was lacking. During the colonial period and even into the republic there was considerable popular feeling against the ownership of agricultural lands by ecclesiastical organizations. Undoubtedly many hearts were gladdened when the Jesuit order was deprived by the royal government of the phenomenally large number of those rich haciendas—as well as urban properties—which it had amassed through the years.

There was surplus farm production even during the colonial period, but most of it reached only local markets. There was little or no large-scale commercial agriculture. The first real opportunity for the development of export production was during the relatively calm political period of the 1860's and 1870's. This short-lived boom, it has already been noted, was brought to an abrupt end by the war with Chile and the subsequent depression. However, it marked the initiation of a new trend that was resumed and expanded with the restoration of relative political and economic stability in the twentieth century. It was at this time that the transition of the coastal economic system from the level of shopkeepers to the level of corporate business began, the same transition that was taking place throughout most of the Western world. With this development, the agriculture of the coast and the pattern of man-land relations were placed in a different context and acquired new meaning. But only in recent decades have the effects of the new economy reached into the sierra, and the more isolated regions have still hardly been touched at all. For this reason it is important to know what technological level is being dealt with when particular aspects of man-land relational patterns are discussed, since their meaning changes in response to changes in the larger system.

Land Distribution on the Coast

(The coastal valleys of Peru have experienced the greatest economic changes in recent times, the obvious reason being their easy accessibility and rich soils. The peculiar physical geography of the coastal strip, though, limits the amount of cultivated land to only slightly more than a million acres. There is more farm land than this in the small and industrial state of Connecticut; there is over one hundred times as much in the state of Texas. Yet the coastal acreage of Peru is highly productive and of great importance to the national economy. About 120,000 acres of the land are planted in sugar cane, and about 321,000 acres in cotton.[1] Rice, which has become an increasingly important coastal crop, is cultivated on about 140,000 coastal acres. These three are generally considered the principal commercial crops, although rice is not exported to any appreciable extent. The rest of the coastal area is devoted to pastures and various food crops, especially maize. Because the land-use is an important factor in the interpretation of land distribution, crop production areas provide logical subdivisions for analyzing the coastal holdings.

Sugar cane production, for example, presents technical problems that rice and cotton do not, in that fairly large units of cultivation are required for profitable operations. At the present time sugar cane is commercially raised in only seven valleys of the coast, mostly in the northern and central regions. Since before the turn of the century the almost constant trend has been to consolidate the separate sugar haciendas into fewer and larger units. One index to this trend is the number of operating sugar mills, which was reduced from thirty-three in 1922 to fifteen in 1950, even though the area cultivated in cane decreased only about 2 per cent in the same period. Another measure of the consolidation trend is the increase in average size of sugar plantations and the concurrent reduction in number. In the sugar-producing Chicama valley of the department of La Libertad, for instance, there were in 1950 four large enterprises, each of which represented the consolidation of numerous smaller farms and haciendas. The hacienda *Cartavio*, owned by W. R. Grace and Company, was cultivating some

10,000 acres of cane and represented the absorption of more than twenty smaller farm units.[2] The holdings of the Empresa Agrícola Chicama, Ltd., owned by the firm of Gildemeister and Company, brought under common ownership more than sixty independent haciendas.[3] This enterprise annually cultivates around 37,000 acres of cane and 12,000 of other food crops.[4] The total area held by the Chicama corporation is in excess of 220 square miles, but this includes thousands of acres of uncultivated and uncultivable lands. The holdings of the other two major haciendas of the Chicama valley are less extensive, but they also have been developed through the consolidation process. In another valley, the Nepeña, in the department of Ancash, 95 per cent of the 60,000 acres of cultivated land has been acquired by the Negociación Azucarera Nepeña, controlled by the commercial firm of A. y F. Wiese, S.A.[5] All these large sugar estates demonstrate the expanding development of corporate farming on the coast. The importance of their enterprise is seen from the fact that in 1947 the value of exported sugar and sugar products constituted approximately 30 per cent of the total value of national exports.[6]

The commercial orientation of the sugar estates has naturally led them to apply such techniques as they have felt would increase production, and in no few instances their application has generated hostility. Modern farm equipment has increased the size of optimum efficiency land units, and the expansion of corporate landholdings has been bitterly resented in some quarters. Even with mechanization manpower requirements for such commercial enterprises are great, and complex systems of social organization of the workers have been developed by the various companies. Vociferous opposition to the social control of laborers has been sounded by various left-wing groups, and the corporations reveal a considerable sensitivity in regard to the issue.

In May of 1950 the author was permitted (after a rather patent probing as to his social and political sentiments) to visit various sugar estates in the Chicama valley through the courtesy of W. R. Grace and Company. A supervised inspection was made of the mill villages of Paramonga, operated by the Grace firm; Casa Grande, of the Empresa Agrícola Chicama; and Chiclín, of Larco Herrera Hermanos en Liquidación. In general, the villages appeared well kept, and the dwellings were far superior in quality to those usually inhabited by agricultural workers on the individually owned haciendas. The workers were supplied with various kinds of Western recreational devices, motion pictures being the most popular. Worker discipline was stringent, by Latin American standards, but not particularly so compared to practices in Europe and the United States. There were no trade unions, and the various managerial forces were unanimous in their militant opposition to union activities. It was their claim, and probably a true one, that union movements were instigated by left-wing political groups. Another managerial charge, that union leaders were the real exploiters of the workers, would have been rather difficult to verify. A few informal interviews about the treatment of workers were ventured in the near-by city of Trujillo. The chief complaint voiced by those who claimed knowledge of the workers' situation was against the rigid discipline, especially at Casa Grande. The managers of the sugar estates answered this charge by pointing out that their workers were better paid and lived in greater physical comfort than those on smaller haciendas. They also resorted to the usual argument that the workers who did not like the conditions were free to go elsewhere.

The policies and practices of the commercial sugar estates in Peru are the standard ones of industries operating under a capitalistic system. They tend to operate in the nineteenth-century tradition of paternalism, but this is not altogether in keeping with their own desires. As industries operating in the southern United States have frequently discovered, workers accustomed to paternalistic management expect it. But with the development of an industrial ethos this attitude of expectation frequently changes to one of resentment. As a speculative observation, it would appear that the workers themselves on the sugar estates are not opposed to the paternalistic treatment which they receive, but the labor leaders—a more sophisticated lot—are. They view it through cynical eyes as sugar-coated exploitation and rail against its proffering and acceptance. The managers seem sincere in their attitudes; they may be misguided, but they are not hypocrites. They do not understand the motives or reasoning of labor leaders. They cannot see why workers should be called upon to oppose managerial policies which, management feels, provide the best living conditions and wages for agricultural workers in the country. So, management in turn accuses the labor leaders of seeking to betray the workers to serve their own occult ends. They earnestly talk of "protecting" their workers from unionism, and there is little doubt that their protection thus far has been thorough. If the experiences of other nations is any guide, though, it is difficult to believe that such a policy, no matter how benevolent its administrators, can long survive the transitional stage of the industrialization process.

Another general observation that might be made of the sugar industry in Peru is that it presents the same question that has confronted every country where capitalistic expansion has taken place, namely, whether the most economically efficient operations are necessarily the most desirable from a social viewpoint. It seems unlikely that there will be agreement on the answer so long as there remain basic differences in the value premises upon which the arguments are based. The yet unsolved problem of monopolistic developments in the United States would indicate that no generally acceptable answer to the question of "bigness" has been provided in the most advanced capitalistic economy in the world. There seems little doubt that the issue will be debated for many years to come, and to an increasing extent in Peru.

Turning to the cultivation of rice and cotton, one finds a different situation. Both crops can be profitably produced on small or large tracts, although certain economic advantages may be gained by increasing the unit area of production.

Cotton is the greatest export crop of Peru, and is cultivated in all parts of twenty-seven of the coastal valleys.[7] About 85 per cent of the production is in the three departments of Piura, Lima, and Ica. The cultivation of rice is largely located in the northern coastal departments of Piura, Lambayeque, and La Libertad, which account for more than three-quarters of the total. The departments of Lima and Arequipa produce another 10 per cent, while the remainder of the production is in other coastal departments and in the selva.[8] Cotton production has shown a general decrease since the peak year of 1938, when nearly

500,000 acres were sown in this crop. The area cultivated in rice, however, increased by 250 per cent between 1915 and 1945. Production quantity more than tripled in the same period as improved cultivation techniques increased yields.[9])

It is almost impossible to say anything of a general nature about land unit sizes in discussing these two crops. Production techniques vary widely from the use of primitive ox-drawn plows to the employment of the latest mechanical equipment. It is not even strictly correct to say that the more primitive methods are used on smaller holdings, since in many cases rather extensive haciendas have been parceled out among a great number of tenants. The best clue to the size of cultivated units is found in Table 7, which shows that in the cotton and rice producing regions, there are relatively few large holdings. This does not preclude the above-mentioned possibility of extensive haciendas being divided up into tenant farms, since each individual enterprise was counted as a separate farm in the tabular presentation.

Very little information is available in regard to coastal farms that do not produce commercial crops. Maize is the most generally grown non-commercial food crop, its area of cultivation on the coast being some 168,000 acres. That is greater than the acreage devoted to all the other food crops combined. With the exception of some few large truck farms near the cities and the sections of the sugar haciendas used for producing food for the workers, nearly all the holdings in food crops are extremely small. Most tenants and some laborers on the larger cotton haciendas utilize small plots of the land to supply their families with food. Systematic market production of such crops is generally lacking; much of the produce seen in the local markets represents merely an excess of foods raised for family consumption.)

It is to be noted also that the extensive use of animal power on coastal farms requires the employment of a considerable area for pasture. The expansion of dairying in recent years suggests that the 1944 estimate of 175,000 acres of pasture land is no longer applicable, but how much the increase has been is unknown.[10] It is not the practice to utilize extensive coastal areas for pasture. One usually finds small units: some are crop lands in rotation; others are permanently in pasture.

The data on farm sizes in the southern coastal departments support the view that small units prevail where the land is used for non-commercial food production and pasture. In the departments of Arequipa, Moquegua, and Tacna, where these types of land utilization predominate, only 15 per cent of the farms are larger than five hectares (12.35 acres). In fact, some of the units are so small that they will not support a farm family, so other means must be found to supplement the farm income.

TABLE 6

IRRIGATED FARM UNITS IN THE PROVINCE OF AREQUIPA
CLASSIFIED BY SIZE, 1950

SIZE CLASSES IN *topos**	FARM UNITS		AREAS	
	Number	Percentage of total	Number in *topos*	Percentage of total
0.1 - 5.0	3,331	71.4	6,915.00	23.4
5.1 - 10.0	653	14.0	4,953.00	16.7
10.1 - 15.0	225	4.8	2,916.00	9.8
15.1 - 20.0	161	3.5	2,917.50	9.9
20.1 - 30.0	159	3.4	4,113.00	13.9
30.1 - 50.0	83	1.8	3,228.75	10.9
50.1 - 100.0	36	0.8	2,428.75	8.2
100.1 - 500.0	15	0.3	2,128.50	7.2
Total:	4,663	100.0	29,600.50	100.0

Source: Perú. Dirección de Aguas e Irrigaciones.
*The *topo* is equivalent to .86 acres.

In 1950, the author made a detailed study of farm land distribution in the province of Arequipa, the results of which are shown in Table 6. Seventy per cent of the farm units were smaller than 5 *topos,* or 4.3 acres, in area. The average size holding was 6.35 *topos,* or approximately 5.5 acres. Only fifteen of the 4,663 farms tabulated were larger than 100 acres, and those made up less than 7 per cent of the total area. As small as these holdings appear, they are still considerably larger than what they were formerly, to judge from a study of the same area made in 1942, which showed the average size unit to be only 3.5 acres.[11]

The only currently available data on size of holdings for the entire coast are tabulations of coastal farm units registered by the Dirección de Aguas e Irrigación. While these are the best materials to be had, the method of tabulation is such that only limited interpretations can be made from them. The tabulations reveal how many farms are in a given size range, but they do not reveal the total acreage of the farms in any given size category. This is no mere statistical ineptitude, since the agricultural economists of the Peruvian Ministry of Agriculture are well trained and were quite aware of the limitations imposed by such a tabulation. Rather, it reflects the general uneasiness of the Peruvian government in circulating figures on such matters for fear that they will serve as ammunition for left-wing political groups.

On the basis of a number of samples from two categories it was roughly estimated that the average-size farm unit in the smallest category was approximately .67 hectares, while the average unit in the 101-500 hectare class was approximately 300 hectares. Assuming these estimates to be reasonably accurate, the total area of the 32,745 units smaller than 6 hectares in size would be 21,939 hectares. Only 723 farms were listed in the 101-500 hectare class, so their total area would be 216,900 hectares, roughly ten times the area of the smallest group. If a minimum of 500 hectares be taken as the unit size for the 195 farms recorded in the "over 500 hectare" category, a minimum total area of 97,500 hectares is computed. Utilizing this extremely conservative figure for comparison, the two largest-unit classes, comprising only 2.2 per cent of the total number of farms, contain together at least fourteen times as much land as the smallest-unit class, which includes 78 per cent of the total number. Clearly, the pattern of farm unit sizes is one of extremes: a great many small holdings that contribute only a small proportion of the total arable area, and relatively few large farms that make up the bulk of the total hectarage. The moderate-size "family farm" unit is notably absent.

LAND DISTRIBUTION IN THE HIGHLANDS

In the sierra an entirely different set of factors operates to produce and give meaning to the land pattern. In the first place, the moun-

TABLE 7

Coastal Farms Classified According to Size by Regions, 1950

SIZE IN HECTARES	NORTH		CENTRAL		SOUTH		TOTAL	
	Number	Per Cent	Number	Per Cent	Number	Per Cent	Number	Per Cent
0 - 5	12,770	74.3	11,386	77.7	8,589	85.5	32,745	78.0
6 - 10	2,154	12.5	1,222	8.3	886	8.8	4,262	10.2
11 - 50	1,671	9.7	1,280	8.8	548	5.4	3,499	8.3
51 - 100	241	1.4	244	1.7	58	.1	543	1.3
101 - 500	285	1.6	412	2.8	26	.1	723	1.7
over 500	84	.5	109	.7	2	.1	195	0.5
Total:	17,205	100.0	14,653	100.0	10,109	100.0	41,967	100.0

Source: Perú, Ministerio de Agricultura, Servicio Cooperativo Inter-Americano de Producción de Alimentos (SCIPA), "Estimación del Número de Empresas agrícolas según su Tamaño" (unpublished study by Division of Economic Studies of SCIPA, February, 1950; mimeographed), p. 2.

tainous terrain has imposed transportation difficulties that have retarded the spread of industrial culture and prevented the development of commercial agriculture to any great extent. A subsistence farming economy is still the prevalent practice, and it is characterized by primitive techniques of cultivation. The few large-scale enterprises are primarily sheep and cattle ranches, with the former type predominating. It is in the sierra that almost the totality of remaining Indian communities is to be found, and, while they have not escaped the influence of European culture by any manner of means, they still bear the cultural stamp of the pre-Hispanic civilization. Their pattern of life, while it may not differ in kind from that of the white and mestizo element, differs sufficiently in degree that it deserves special consideration.

(In the sierra the relationships between land use and size of holdings can be traced only along the most general and obvious lines. Ranching enterprises, for example, of necessity require larger holdings than are necessary for crop cultivation. Particularly in the high sierra, where natural pasture is scanty and cultivation virtually impossible, each animal requires a number of hectares of grazing land. What appear to be tremendous holdings in terms of area, therefore, may in actuality represent extremely modest ranches in terms of the actual stock they can carry.)

Food crops are another consideration. The great staple of the sierra is the potato, of which there are hundreds of varieties. In fact, Peru is generally credited as being the original locale of the so-called "Irish" potato. It is conservatively estimated that more than 400,000 acres of potatoes are cultivated in the sierra, for the most part on small plots and with crude techniques. Another tuberous plant, the *camote,* and yucca are grown on an estimated 170,000 acres. Most of the 750,-000 acres of wheat and barley grown in Peru is produced on sierra farms, as are the native grains *quinua* and *canihua,* which are sown on an estimated 110,000 acres. Maize is cultivated throughout the region, but there are no accurate data as to acreage or production. The area of cultivated pasture in the sierra probably does not exceed that of the coast, but natural pasture is to be measured in millions of acres. Since almost all the sierra crops are grown on a subsistence basis, there is little correlation between the particular types of crops and the sizes of land units.

The data on general land distribution in the sierra are even less adequate than those available for the coast, and more difficult to interpret. There are, for example, more than five times as many sierra farms larger than 500 hectares as there are coastal farms in this size category, but many of these extensive sierra farms contain vast expanses of uncultivable land. It would be a difficult task to ascertain how many of these large holdings in the sierra are relatively unproductive because of topography, soil, and climate, and how many are potentially productive but inefficiently operated. The latter type conforms more closely to the traditional concept of a latifundium, and it is apparent that some such do exist in the Peruvian highlands. As in the colonial period, cultivation is done by Indian laborers who eke out a bare subsistence while the landlords (often absentee) receive small profits, which are possible only because of the low operating cost.

In many of the Indian communities the other size extreme of land holdings is to be found. Frequently the population has increased several fold while the lands of the community have either remained the same size or even diminished. The result has been continuous subdivision of family plots until the individual units are almost microscopic. It is not rare to find an individual's share of the more fertile community lands measured in terms of one or two furrows.[12] One case is cited in the SCIPA publication *La Situación Alimenticia en el Perú*, in which no fewer than two hundred persons cultivated strips of a three-hectare plot that had been irrigated. In the same sierra province there were six villages populated by 3,100 farmers and their families. No farmer owned more than one hectare of farm land.[13]

\The coexistence of extremely large and extremely small holdings such as occurs in Peru is not unusual. If the agricultural population is large, land limited, and a considerable portion of the land held in large blocks, the probability is high that the remainder of the land will be greatly subdivided. In Peru this process of subdivision is furthered by the custom of bequeathing equal land shares to heirs. As plots become too small to yield a livelihood, the owners are forced either to work as laborers on near-by large holdings or to migrate. The strong desire of many of the Indians to cultivate their own holdings leads to their choice of the former alternative. In this manner the large haciendas are assured a constant, if not efficient, labor supply which is cheap enough to make operations profitable, thus serving to perpetuate the system./

The distribution of farm units by size for the sierra is shown in Table 8. The tabulations shown have the same limitations as those for coastal holdings, plus a few more of their own which further reduce their reliability and utility. The major ones are that the source of the data is a tax-collecting agency of the government, and that the sierra farms are considerably more inaccessible than those of the coast. It is probable that many of the farm units have not been recorded and that the recorded sizes, particularly of the larger units, are smaller than the true sizes. Even so, the distributional relationships may be roughly computed. The average size of the smallest units, based on a crude sampling, was 1.62 hectares. Thus the total area of the 16,978 farms under six hectares in size may be estimated at 27,504 hectares. If the average and minimum sizes of 300 and 500 hectares, respectively, are again chosen as the unit areas of the two largest-unit categories of farms, the total area of the 2,605 units in these two classes is at least 1,021,100 hectares. Using the most conservative figures again, we find that the two largest groups of units, making up 9.9 per cent of the numerical total, contain over thirty-seven times as much land as the smallest group, into which 64.6 per cent of the total number of units fall. The pattern of distribution resembles very closely that of the coast, but it does not have the same meaning. The concentration of ownership on the coast represents the expansiveness of capitalistic enterprise; that of the sierra represents the survival of the colonial latifundium. Until the fundamental differences in these two types of "bigness" are understood, rational approaches to the solving of the social and economic problems associated with each will be virtually impossible.

TABLE 8

Sierra Farms Classified According to Size by Regions, 1950

SIZE IN HECTARES	NORTH		CENTRAL		SOUTH		TOTAL	
	Number	Per Cent	Number	Per Cent	Number	Per Cent	Number	Per Cent
0 - 5	3,365	46.3	6,657	75.4	6,956	68.5	16,978	64.6
6 - 10	890	12.2	428	4.8	920	9.0	2,238	8.5
11 - 50	1,926	26.5	827	9.4	813	8.0	3,566	13.6
51 - 100	466	6.4	261	2.9	164	1.6	891	3.4
101 - 500	368	5.1	431	4.9	608	5.9	1,407	5.3
over 500	256	3.5	232	2.6	710	7.0	1,198	4.6
Total:	7,271	100.0	8,836	100.0	10,171	100.0	26,278	100.0

Source: Perú, Ministerio de Agricultura, SCIPA, "Estimación del Número de Empresas Agrícolas según su Tamaño" (unpublished study by Division of Economic Studies of SCIPA, February, 1950; mimeographed), p. 3.

68

LAND DISTRIBUTION AND POPULATION GROWTH

Many of the problems of land distribution in Peru, it has been seen, stem from the sheer lack of arable land. On the basis of current estimates, the amount of cultivated land per inhabitant is less than half an acre, a fact that is alleviated to some extent by the possibility of producing several crops a year in many localities. On the other hand, the situation is complicated by the direct dependence of such a large proportion of the population upon agriculture and the unequal distribution of the cultivable land among them. Furthermore, it is clearly evident that the population has increased much faster than new areas can be brought under cultivation, so the ratio of land to population has continued to shrink. On the coast, for example, irrigation projects increased the amount of cultivable land by about 15 per cent during the period from 1900 to 1940.[14] During the same time the national population increased an estimated 84 per cent, of which the coastal cities received a disproportionately large share.[15] On the coast the food demand has been met to some extent by the application of improved agricultural techniques which have increased yields, but these have not penetrated to many sections of the sierra. In the highlands, under conditions of equalized distribution, each farm family would have about four acres of cultivated land.[16] Since such land is not equally distributed, it is clearly apparent that many families have the most minute holdings or none at all.

The direct and indirect consequences of land scarcity in Peru can be traced almost endlessly in terms of high rents, low per capita production, low wages for farm labor, lack of purchasing power for the masses, absence of a strong domestic market for manufactured goods, and retarded industrial development.[17] It should be clearly recognized, however, that the consideration of some of these consequences as problem conditions is valid only under the standards of an industrial culture. The masses lacked purchasing power under the Inca regime also; but in a system where units are for the most part self-sustaining the relative absence of money or other media of exchange is of little importance. When the operation of the economic system is dependent upon specialization and commerce, it is necessary that surplus production be maintained. The manufacturers cannot sell to the farmers if the farmers produce only enough to meet their own needs. The current situation in Peru, however, is more serious than the mere lack of a surplus: in many cases the farmers on their reduced holdings and with their present cultivation practices are not producing enough food to meet even their own needs. Hence, in recent years critical food shortages have developed, requiring the importation of food products at a time when the nation badly needs machinery and other durable goods if its own industries are to develop. There is no intention here of attributing such a situation to any single factor, but it would appear irrefutable that land scarcity, complicated by the scheme of distribution, must be considered of basic importance.

LAND DISTRIBUTION AND THE TENURE SYSTEM

Land distribution patterns and tenure practices are interdependent variables, as the Peruvian agrarian situation well illustrates. What particularly complicates the relationships in Peru is the preservation of aspects of both the indigenous and the Hispanic man-land systems, plus the introduction of a few unique features resulting from the synthesis. Through the course of years the trend of increasing western- ization seems definitely to have been established, with earlier practices prevailing only in the remaining Indian communities. But even these latter have felt the impact of European ideas to a marked extent.

The unremitting transfer of Peruvian agricultural lands to Spanish hands left little recourse for the dispossessed Indians except to work for those who had gained control. The white *hacendados,* needing labor, which they were not willing or able to provide personally, adopted the classic practice which Carl Brinkman has so ably described: "Even the most consistently developed large-scale farming of the present time, while premising to some extent the labor supply of a landless proletariat, tends nevertheless to replace former limitations on the personal freedom of the cultivators by giving them some hold on the land, even if it be only a plot, a cottage, or a share in the raw produce."[18] He could well have been describing the relationship between the Spanish landowners and the Indian *yanaconas.* The latter, in many cases, never bothered to move from the lands which they once possessed, but simply passed into the service of the new owner. In other cases they fled from the colonial *reducciones* because of even worse conditions which prevailed in many of them and sought refuge on the haciendas. There they were allowed to till for their own subsistence, in exchange for which they labored gratuitously for the *hacendado*.

Large holdings, it should be re-emphasized, serve to perpetuate themselves by the mere fact of their existence. In the case of Peru, as in all other countries where distribution patterns of this nature exist, the landless and near-landless are forced to hire out as laborers if they are to survive. While they may be paid in cash, more frequently their remuneration is simply the right to utilize an unassigned portion of the owner's land for their own purposes. It is rare when the plot is sufficiently large or fertile to provide more than a bare sustenance for their families. The following is from an official report of farm conditions on lands newly brought into cultivation in 1943 through irrigation projects in the department of Arequipa:

Instead of dividing the Siguas irrigation development into family-sized farm units, the bulk of this area, namely, three-fourths of it, [was] divided into units considerably larger than could be operated efficiently by a farm family. Furthermore, these units are generally owned and operated by absentee landlords. The balance of the area, about one fourth of the total, is divided into very small units with the hope of having in the area farm laborers who would have excess time to work on the large holdings. This method of dividing merely perpetuates the problem which has persisted in the area for a long time.[19]

Seen in such a light, part of the relationship between land distribution and tenure assumes a new clarity. The large holdings tend to create their own tenants and laborers, without which they could not continue in operation. As long as the rural proletarian families continue to increase in number while the land supply remains limited, the pattern is likely to continue.

4.

Land Tenure Systems

LAND TENURE SYSTEMS are the interrelated assignments of differential rights to land possession and use. In most agrarian societies there are more land users than there are landowners. As a consequence, tenancy arrangements are developed through which those who own land allow others to occupy and utilize it in exchange for goods or some service. The variety of such arrangements is wide, but certain basic patterns tend to recur in time and space. This suggests that fundamental types develop as general responses to particular combinations of various factors and sociocultural processes. One of the aims of a social science is to arrive at general rules that express the likelihood that a given combination of factors and processes will produce a given result. At the present time, however, the studies of comparative land systems are inadequate to justify more than some rather limited and relatively simple generalizations.

The supply of land and distribution of possession rights to it within any given society will largely determine the extent of tenancy arrangements, but these factors do not dictate what these arrangements will be. Factors other than supply and distribution appear to be of greater significance in the choice of specific forms. These other variables include the social structure of the population, the power relations between landed and landless, the technological level of the culture, the presence or absence of operating capital, and the uses to which the land is put. The coexistence of different types of arrangements under more or less identical conditions suggests that when several equal alternatives are possible, the final decision is likely to be determined by non-rational considerations. Tradition will generally play a leading part in the selection of an arrangement in any area where established practices have developed, even where other factors might suggest a more suitable arrangement, for the simple reason that the parties involved feel more security in entering agreements with familiar terms. It is not unusual to find tenants preferring a traditional arrangement with relatively unfavorable terms to a more favorable but newer form with which they have not had experience.

In Peru, as in many other Latin American countries, there are still two basic types of land tenure stemming from separate cultural systems. One type, it has been noted, is rooted in the collective society of the Indians; the other, in the individualistic society of the Spanish. The latter is clearly predominant at the present time, but the remaining differences are sufficiently great to justify their separate analysis. Before such an analysis is made, it will be worth while to look at the data on tenure collected by the Peruvian census of 1940, the pertinent materials being reproduced in Table 9.

The collection of tenure data on a national basis through the 1940

TABLE 9

NUMBER AND PERCENTAGE OF POPULATION EMPLOYED IN AGRICULTURE,
RANCHING, STOCK BREEDING, FORESTRY, HUNTING, AND FISHING,
CLASSIFIED BY OCCUPATIONAL CATEGORIES, 1940

TENURE CLASS	AGRICULTURE		RANCHING, STOCK BREEDING, HUNTING, AND FISHING	
	Number	Percentage	Number	Percentage
Landlords and owners	510,302	39.5	41,749	16.5
Employees	4,021	.3	1,205	.5
Laborers	338,792	26.1	162,551	64.2
Family workers	272,788	21.1	26,765	10.6
Independents	161,192	12.5	19,532	7.8
Undeclared	6,119	.5	1,173	.4
Total:	1,293,214	100.0	252,975	100.0

Source: Censo nacional . . . 1940, I, 410-411, cuadro 116; 412-413, cuadro 117.

census was the first attempt of its kind in Peru. Unfortunately, the tabulated materials have shortcomings which invalidate them for purposes of detailed analysis. One of the more serious faults is the lack of clear definitions for tenure categories. It is impossible to tell from the census data, for example, how the Indians who live in the agrarian communities have been classified in regard to tenure. Another feature that limits the utility of the census materials is that the tabulations include over 50,000 children aged six through fourteen years engaged in agriculture, and more than 60,000 in animal husbandry enterprises.[1] The children listed as agriculturalists have possibly been included also in the category of family workers, but this is evidently not true for the other group, where the total number listed as family workers is less than 27,000. There is no justification given for classifying some 33,000 children under fifteen years of age as independent laborers or in some other tenure class.

One of the more interesting aspects of the census materials is the exceedingly high percentage of landlords and owners within the total group. This proportion would have been even higher had only adults been enumerated, since it is doubtful that many of the children were listed in the owner class. Caution must be exercised in the interpretation of these figures, however, because there is no indication of how tenure classifications were made in those cases of individuals falling into two or more categories. For example, many persons who were the possessors of diminutive plots may have listed themselves as owners or landlords even though their principal source of livelihood was employment as farm laborers on the holdings of others. The prestige associated with landownership is sufficient motivation for such a misleading claim. Furthermore, with less than four million cultivated acres in all Peru, and with these unequally distributed, there seems to be ample evidence that some of the half million persons claiming to be landlords and owners had holdings that were too small to yield them a subsistence income.

Other data from the census that appear questionable are those on tenancy. Renters, classified as "independents" in the census tabulations, constitute only a small proportion of the enumerated total, yet various forms of tenancy are widely practiced in Peru. Sharecroppers are far too numerous to have been included in the category of "independents," so presumably they were listed as laborers. There is no indication of how other forms of tenancy were categorized. The author interviewed a number of Peruvian census officials in an attempt to clarify this matter, but met with little success. A plausible explanation would seem to be that many tenants were also owners, and preferred to be listed in the higher prestige class. Despite its deficiencies, this pioneer effort to collect tenure information makes a major contribution in its revelation of the truly great number of agriculturists in Peru who claim to be landowners.

The development of a taxonomy of tenure rights in Peru offers a number of conceptual challenges, not all of which, it is regrettably reported, have been met. The first difficulty has already been noted— that of reconciling within one scheme practices which developed from two disparate sources. This is the same problem in the abstract that Peru faces in reality, and there appears no logical way to integrate incompatible forms. On the other hand, the separate classification of the practices which are traceable to the pre-Hispanic collective system is not completely justifiable, although it has been done, because of the obvious alterations effected by Spanish individualistic influences.

A second difficulty encountered in the attempt to classify tenancy practices lies in the use of different colloquial names for what are more or less the same basic arrangements. Nor is this the only semantic confusion. The same name in different localities referred to entirely different practices. A *colono* in the sierra, for example, is not the same thing as a *colono* on the coast; he corresponds more to the coastal *yanacona,* while the coastal *colono* is frequently called a *partidario* in the sierra. This problem has finally been resolved by the decision to avoid local terms altogether, except in parenthetical reference, and to use verbal or written contract terms as the means of identifying tenant classes. In this manner the following classification system has been derived, based on source materials secured through field observations, interviews, and various published and unpublished works on the subject:

I. Non-operating owners
   A. Individuals and commercial corporations
   B. National and local governmental bodies
   C. Religious, charitable, and educational institutions

II. Owner-operators
   A. Individuals
   B. Commercial firms and incorporated estates

III. Non-owner operators
   A. Administrators
   B. Renters
      1. Cash renters (and labor)
      2. Standing renters (and labor)
      3. Combinations cash and standing renters
         (and labor)
   C. Sharecroppers
      1. Produce share only
      2. Produce share and labor

IV. Farm laborers
   A. Paid in cash (and rations)
   B. Paid in land usufruct
   C. Paid in combinations of cash, rations, and land
      usufruct
   D. Unpaid family laborers

V. *Comuneros*
   A. Usufructuaries of community land
   B. Landowners with maintenance of community
      practices
   C. Combinations of private ownership and usufruct of
      community land

This outline, despite its inadequacies, does offer a guide for a more complete descriptive analysis of land rights in contemporary Peru.

NON-OPERATING OWNERS

Absentee ownership is still widespread in Peru, but there are no statistical clues as to its incidence. This pattern was established during the colonial period, when landownership accorded prestige but farming as an occupation did not, and has continued, although considerably diminished, until the present. In 1925 W. E. Dunn reported:

Most of the large landowners live in Lima or in the provincial capitals, leaving the actual administration of the estate to an overseer (*mayordomo*). The proprietors are frequently professional men, who give little attention to their property so long as it yields a satisfactory income. Overseers are often poorly paid and must indulge in questionable practices in order to supplement their income. Under such conditions, progressive methods are almost unknown.[2]

The main change that has occurred since Dunn's report has been a general increase in the interest shown by landowners in farming operations as a market economy has developed more fully.

In some cases, particularly on the coast, landowners have found it more profitable to lease their lands to commercial enterprisers than to try to operate them either directly or indirectly themselves. Prior to World War II a number of Japanese agricultural firms had leased such lands in the rich coastal valleys and were, from all accounts, achieving considerable financial success. They were doing so well, in fact, that many who had leased their estates welcomed the opportunity provided by the war to retrieve them and go into business themselves.

Another type of commercial firm which has developed within recent times is that formed by the heirs to some estate. Frequently the land is leased by the corporation thus formed to one of the heirs or to other persons, with the family stockholders receiving the rent as dividends. In other cases the corporation may prefer to operate the estate through an administrator, who may or may not be one of the family members. Then the heirs split profits instead of rents.

Contrary to situations existing in other countries, good farm lands in Peru are considered a relatively safe investment. For that reason, many non-farm corporations will invest in good agricultural lands in preference to other types of securities. Naturally, they must exercise care in the choice of tenants; but land taxes are low and the demand so high that a steady income from such investments seems assured.

Governing bodies from local municipalities on up to the national government own a considerable, but unknown, amount of agricultural and grazing lands in Peru. Many of the municipal holdings date back to the *ejidos, propios,* and *dehesas* of the colonial towns. These are generally not large holdings; they are leased by the *cabildos* to augment municipal budgets. Provincial councils, which correspond roughly to county commissions in the United States, also have lands which are rented theoretically to the highest bidder. The national government leases pasturage rights on some of the public domain suitable for that purpose.

In July of 1949, the national administration issued a decree ordering the expropriation of all unimproved lands (*terrenos eriazos*) whose owners failed to comply with government specifications for improvements.[3] The ostensible purpose of this measure was to allow the government to carry out a land program to bring new areas under cultivation and to reclaim deteriorated agricultural lands. The reclaimed lands were then, presumably, to be redistributed to private purchasers. Whatever may have been the intention of the decree, nothing ever came of it because of the vociferous opposition of the landowners at whom it was directed.

Religious institutions still control a great amount of land in Peru, although not so much as they once did. In general, such lands are distributed among numerous small holdings of various churches, parishes, and other ecclesiastical bodies. The quantity is great only when considered in the totality, and there are no statistical data available on this subject. The best study to date on these lands is that made by Julio Delgado in the late 1920's.[4] Delgado classified the lands into those of churches, parishes, saints, and monastic orders. The rents from the church lands (*bienes del templo*) are used to defray normal operating expenses. The rents of the parish lands (*parroquiales*) help provide the salaries of the priests. The lands of the saints (*tierras del santo*) are rented to pay for the expenses of the fiesta held on the day of the saint to whom the land "belongs." Sometimes, instead of being rented, the saints' lands are assigned to volunteers or appointees, who are expected to bear all fiesta expenses in return. Frequently these expenses are far greater than the cash realization from the cultivation of the land. Lands of convents and monasteries are usually rented to pay general expenses of those organizations. It is not uncommon that these properties have been donated by the faithful or presented as dowries upon the entrance of some landowner's daughter into a convent.

Charitable institutions (*beneficencias*) derive a considerable proportion of their income from lands which were donated by private individuals or by early government administrations. Some of these charitable organizations trace the ownership of their lands to colonial grants. During the three-year period 1944 through 1946 some eighty *beneficencias* received a total annual income of more than three million *soles* from the rental of their properties, a source which accounted for about 13 per cent of their budgets.[5]

Both public and private educational institutions own lands of various sorts, the rentals from which contribute to their upkeep. This means of supporting public and semipublic institutions dates from colonial days when land was relatively plentiful and the most stable source of revenue. Such a system is not without its disadvantages, many of which are common to all forms of absentee ownership when the owner is primarily interested in other activities. Not infrequently the cost of litigation borne by institutions that are trying to collect unpaid rents or evict undesirable tenants consumes a large share of the profits.[6]

The effects of granting lands to ecclesiastic organizations soon became apparent to the colonial government, and numerous laws were directed toward the restraint of any further land acquisitions by such bodies. This restrictive policy was continued into the republic. It will be remembered that Bolívar issued decrees in 1825 prohibiting the transfer of land into mortmain. This still did not put any of the lands that had already been acquired by these institutions back into circulation. The Constitution of 1828 declared the right of ecclesiastic institutions to dispose of their lands, but little use was made of this privilege. Later legislation in 1901 and 1907 finally made it possible for educational and religious institutions to sell their lands with relative ease. Another law in 1920 required *beneficencias* to distribute their property leases more equitably than had been their practice. As a result of this legislation, which reflected growing public opinion in opposition to the amassing of agricultural lands by such institutions, much land was transferred back to private hands. There are no available materials as to the extent of this circulation, but numerous instances have been recorded of villagers who demanded and received the right to purchase parochial and church lands.

The author's study of land distribution in the province of Arequipa revealed that religious institutions owned twenty-eight separate, and small, plots of land that constituted slightly over 4 per cent of the total area under investigation. Hospitals and *beneficencias* owned fourteen plots, containing 2 per cent of the total area; municipal and provincial governments and the various schools altogether possessed twenty-two plots, making up about 1 per cent of the entirety. Unfortunately, it is impossible to say how typical this case is. From personal observations and interviews with persons acquainted with various local situations, it would appear that ownership of 5 to 10 per cent of the cultivated land around towns by such institutions is not an unreasonable estimate.

OWNER-OPERATORS

To judge from the census figures, most farms in Peru are operated by their owners, in spite of the prevalence of absentee ownership. It is clearly apparent that the reason for this is that most farm units are extremely small and easily cultivated by a single family. Whether most of the farm area is cultivated directly by the owners is not so easily ascertained. If we include commercial agricultural enterprises within the category of owner-operators, then we can probably answer the implied question in the affirmative. This would raise the question, though, as to whether the real owners, i.e., the stockholders of the corporations, technically operate the haciendas. The justification offered for including commercial agricultural firms in the class of owner-operators is that they are quite distinct from the class of individual and corporate owners that is interested primarily in rental income and plays no part in the production process.

Forty per cent of the economically active population engaged in agriculture claimed to be landowners, according to the 1940 census figures previously cited. It can be assumed, because of the great number of small holdings, that most of these claimants actually cultivated their own lands. In addition, many of them probably helped cultivate lands which they did not own. On the coast and near urban regions recent industrial development has given work opportunities to many of those whose holdings are too small to provide a living, so that they constitute a growing class of small part-time farmers.

Large commercial farms in Peru have developed for the most part in the twentieth century. Some of the proprietor firms are owned by a relatively few individuals, while others sell stock on the open market. In some cases, such as the larger sugar estates, the agricultural organizations are subsidiaries of more extensive commercial and industrial corporations.

The incorporation of estates for operation as business enterprises by the heirs has already been mentioned. Basically, this is a device for preventing the fragmentation of large holdings which would otherwise take place under Peruvian inheritance statutes. This is the same function served by the colonial entail, or *mayorazgo,* except that an entailed estate went to only one of the heirs. The corporate form makes it possible for all the heirs to receive shares in the form of stock, while the estate remains intact.

Nearly all the larger commercial farms are located in coastal valleys, but in recent years there has been a tendency for them to spread to the sierra. This has been particularly true in ranching developments. The best indication of the number of such firms in operation is the membership roll of the Sociedad Nacional Agraria, an association maintained to further the interests of commercial agriculture. About three hundred corporations are listed among the members of the S.N.A., which probably includes all the more important ones.

NON-OWNER OPERATORS

The numerous types of arrangement that exist between landlords and tenants make a classification of non-owner operators a difficult task. In fact, the local variations are so great that it would require an entire volume to catalog them, so those which are described in the following passages must be considered only basic types, which differ in detail according to local customs. It should be remembered, also, that agriculturists are not restricted to any tenure class and may concurrently hold several tenure statuses, such as owner-operator, tenant, and laborer, in relation to different farm units.

In the first class of non-owner operators may be listed farm administrators, or managers. These are distinguished from other types in the general category in that their positions are salaried, so their income is not directly dependent upon production. Indirectly, of course, there is a relationship, since the manager who does not live up to the production expectations of the owner will probably be replaced. Administrative types vary from the *mayordomos* of individually owned haciendas to staff members of complex commercial farm organizations. In the case of the former, frequently the only distinguishable difference between the *mayordomo* and the laborer is in the matter of delegated responsibility and authority. Some *mayordomos* may stay with a single family or hacienda for decades; others change positions nearly every year. For many of the landless this position represents the top rung of the agricultural ladder.

The administrative staffs of the large commercial farms are of a different order because of their specialized functions. The directors and subdirectors of the farming operations are trained technicians, and only the field overseers could be compared in terms of their operations to the *mayordomos*. As salaried professionals the administrative personnel operate under written contracts, another feature which distinguishes them from the average manager of a small hacienda. In the final analysis, the basic distinction between the two types of administrator lies in the number and type of farm operations which each must supervise. These increase in complexity through specialization of techniques and equipment. The managers of commercial farms must possess knowledge of a wide range of technical skills. Such men are difficult to replace and hence command good salaries.

Proceeding to the non-owner operator class of renters, one finds a situation difficult to analyze clearly because the practice of renting is still in a state of evolution in many sections. Renting was seldom practiced in the pre-Hispanic period, so far as is known; it was introduced on a wide scale with the system of private enterprise. Yet the systems of renting as practiced in Peru reflect more than the mere dispersion of a particular cultural trait. More accurately, they represent a compromise between the conquering Spanish and the conquered Indians in regard to the use of the agricultural lands. The former could reap no wealth from the seized lands without the labor of the latter; neither could the Indians continue in their agrarian way of life without some access to the fields. The resulting compromise was possible only because of the particular attitudes toward the land held by the different cultural groups. Had the Spanish placed high value on the practice of cultivation as such and come over in sufficient numbers to establish thousands of small agricultural villages (as the Spanish throne apparently desired, to judge from the Ordinances of Population), it is not improbable that the natives would have been completely eradicated. Had the Indian element not felt the strong compulsion to till the fields, or had it been as recalcitrant as the North American Indians in its attitude toward forced labor, it is also doubtful that any such compromise solution would have been attained.

As a consequence of the early situation, plus factors introduced at a later period, there has never been any clear line of demarcation between tenants who pay a portion of their rent in labor and laborers who are partly paid in the allowed use of an assigned plot of land. From a historical point of view, the colonial *hacendados* considered their *yanaconas* as laborers who lived on the land and were allowed to cultivate a part of it for their own subsistence. There is no indication that they were thought of as tenants, so the practice of renting can be considered a later development. In another sense, the development of renting is indicative of status rise on the part of the landless, or at least some of them. Nevertheless, the continued practices of owners paying laborers with tillage rights and of tenants paying part of their rent with labor are in many cases so nearly identical that any division between them would appear arbitrary.

The system of cash renting, which may be thought of as a more refined form of tenancy in that a stipulated amount of money is paid for the use of a given plot of land for a specified length of time, appears to have been introduced by the Spanish; it is not a synthetic development, as are some of the other types of land-leasing arrangements. Cash renting as practiced in Peru, however, is not so refined that written contracts are always used, despite a legal specification to that effect as part of the rental laws of 1947.[7] In general, the use of verbal contracts reflects the traditional advantageous position of landlords. The rental laws of 1947 favored tenants by establishing maximum rental fees and minimum lease periods. Had they been enforced, they would have definitely increased the bargaining power of the landless in Peru. But it was practically a foregone conclusion at the time of their passage that they would not be enforced, because of the political power of landlords. Upon inquiry in 1950 the author found not only that the law was not being enforced but that many landlords who had previously used written contracts had reverted to informal contracts because they were not willing to accept the formal provisions which would have been required by the 1947 laws. A study of land laws in Peru from the earliest colonial times to the present would suggest that the most likely way to perpetuate a particular practice is to pass a law forbidding it.

More popular than cash renting in Peru is the practice of paying a standing rent for the land—that is, payment in the form of a stated amount of the principal crop. On the coast this practice is known as *yanaconaje*. As previously mentioned, the standing renters of the sierra go under other names such as *colonos* and *partidarios,* but the practice is basically the same. The reason for the popularity of this rental system on the coast is that it is particularly suited to cotton cultivation. When the commercial possibilities of that crop began to be realized in the mid-nineteenth century, *hacendados* frequently found that the most efficient method of production was to apportion the various fields of the hacienda among *yanaconas* who carried out the actual cultivation. The arrangement was usually a simple verbal agreement under which the *yanacona* undertook to cultivate the assigned field and pay as rent a specified number of quintals of cotton. The proprietor, for his part, advanced the *yanacona* an outfit, known as the *habilitación,* consisting of tools, oxen, seeds, fertilizer, and other necessary equipment. In some cases the tenant was furnished with the cash to buy the outfit, although this was less common. The *habilitación* was repaid with interest at the end of the year from the *yanacona*'s cotton which remained after payment of the rent. Frequently the landlord was obliged to make other loans before the harvest, and these were also repaid with interest from the crop.

Under such an arrangement most of the advantages lay with the proprietor. If, for example, any disagreement arose as to the terms of the verbal contract, the proprietor's version was the accepted one. The landlord also made the decision as to what the standing rent should be, basing it on his estimate of what the land should produce. Sometimes, particularly in bad years, the rent accounted for almost the entirety of the crop. Some proprietors, also, were prone to charge excessive interest rates on the *habilitaciones,* and it was common practice for haciendas to maintain their own commissaries (*almacenes*) from which the *yanaconas* were forced to buy goods at higher than market price. The tenant, being obliged to plant what was stipulated by the owner, had little control over his crop. Sometimes he was forced to sell to the owner what remained after the deduction of rent, equipment, loans, and interest, at a price generally lower than the market quotation, in order to be assured of a lease the following year.

Theoretically, the *yanacona* paid for the use of the land with the specified crop stand, but traditionally he had additional obligations. If the proprietor cultivated a portion of the *hacienda* himself rather than leasing it all to tenants, the *yanaconas* were commonly expected to provide labor for a certain number of days each month, either gratuitously or for less than the prevailing wage. In other instances the tenant was required to make permanent improvements upon his rented portion of the land, for which he received no remuneration. A disastrous year could bind an individual to the same hacienda for several more years beyond the specified contract period in order to free himself from the incurred debt. The proprietor, however, could evict the tenant almost at will, since the latter had no recourse to law courts because of the lack of any written agreements. But it should not be thought that all tenants operating under the system of *yanaconaje* were exploited simply because exploitation was possible; neither should it be thought that the tenants were always sinned against and never sinning.

Viewed analytically, the system of *yanaconaje* in Peru developed in response to a situation somewhat similar to that which existed in the southern United States following the War Between the States. The primary social and economic factors which operated to produce this situation in Peru were: (1) the relative shortage of agricultural land; (2) the lack of working capital on the part of both landowners and tenants; (3) the desire of the landowners to assure themselves of a labor force through binding the workers to the soil; (4) the preference of the Indian and mestizo tenants for cultivating a plot of their own rather than working as laborers with no personal attachment to the land; and (5) the pattern of social relations existing between white proprietors and Indian or mestizo tenants.

Some further comment might be made about this social pattern, because it is not unlike that formerly observed between white plantation owners and Negro tenants in the South, or, for that matter, between owners and tenants from different social groups in many sections of the world. The most obvious characteristic is the unquestioned assumption of superiority on the part of the owner and its acceptance on the part of the tenant. Throughout the decades Peruvian *hacendados* have complained about the general inefficiency of their Indian tenants. Yet when Oriental laborers, who did work efficiently and at low wages, moved in, the cries of anguish rose in unprecedented volume. A major reason for this would seem to be that the traditional pattern of social relationships was changed even though the economic arrangements were basically unaltered. Certainly the loudly voiced charge that the Orientals were ruining the level of living of the Peruvian Indians seems ridiculous when the relative economic stagnation of the latter group is considered. What probably stimulated the sudden solicitude of the landowners for their Indians is that they saw in the industrious and parsimonious Orientals a competitive threat that the native tenants were never likely to present.

Yanaconaje is still practiced in many regions, but it has been modified as tenants operating under the system have gained status. Some of the modifications have developed as a result of lawsuits waged against abusive practices. Until recently, however, there was little legislation for the protection of either *yanaconas* or proprietors. For some reason, the system received no consideration in the Civil Code articles which regulated other tenancy arrangements. An attempt to legislate in this neglected area was made with the so-called *Law of Yanaconaje,* passed in 1947 under the liberal Bustamante administration. The main provisions of the law were that all contracts should be written and that they could not include clauses obliging the *yanacona* to sell his crop excess to the owner, to contribute free work not in connection with his own land, to make permanent improvements without compensation, or to trade obligatorily with the commissary of the proprietor. The law also called for a reduction of the fixed rent in case of crop failure over which the tenant had no control, and established a minimum lease term of three years. The tenant was accorded preferential rights in the event the proprietor continued to lease his property after the expiration of the original contract. A maximum rent not to exceed 6 per cent of the assessed value of the property was set, and it was further stipulated that the interest rate on the *habilitación* could not legally exceed 12 per cent. The proprietor was required to furnish a house for the tenant or to pay for one which the tenant himself constructed. Further provisions of the law specified the grounds for the termination of the contract and provided that cases of dispute should be submitted for arbitration.[8]

Suffice it to say, the *Law of Yanaconaje* was never enforced. This was due partly to the opposition of the landowners and partly to defects in the law itself. One of these was the basing of rents upon assessed property value, such value being a controversial matter at best. The immediate reaction to the promulgation of the law was that owners sought to evict their tenants rather than to comply with its provisions. The tenants retaliated with countersuits, and within a few months the courts were flooded. Finally a decree law was issued by the military junta which had meanwhile seized control, prohibiting the initiation of eviction trials and virtually suspending further application of the measure.[9] As a result, conditions returned to their previous state.

Even though it was not effectively applied, the very fact that the *Law of Yanaconaje* was passed at all is indicative of the growing power of the tenantry. Their rise may be accounted for partly by the rise of commercial agriculture and the consequent increased importance of good tenants, and partly by the enlistment of some political leaders on the side of the tenants in a bid for power. In response to this threat landlords have tended to make voluntary concessions to their tenants, possibly in the hope of thus forestalling legislation.

Another form of rental arrangement in Peru, which is less commonly practiced than cash or stand renting, is one in which the renters pay various combinations of cash and produce. In general, this practice seems to be a variation of *yanaconaje,* in which *yanaconas* who formerly contributed fixed amounts of labor to the farm of their landlord as part of their rent are allowed to pay the cash equivalent of this labor. This probably explains the rarity of the practice, since few *yanaconas* possess sufficient cash to make the substitution. It is still a common practice for landowners to rent part of their holdings for the sole purpose of obtaining the labor of the tenants, so labor stipulations are found in all types of contracts, regardless of how the rest of the rent is paid.

There is considerable evidence that the tenancy arrangements which have developed in Peru have often operated to the detriment of the land and agriculture. The prevalence of short-term contracts means that there are few areas where tenants feel sufficiently secure to expend the extra effort needed to make permanent improvements on the farm or even to protect what is already there. Such an attitude has led to erosion and soil depletion in many regions, with resultant decreased production and increased production costs. An additional, but frequently overlooked, drain on rural economy traceable to renting practices is the cost of the innumerable lawsuits which have developed from landlord-tenant disputes. Neither can the general social unrest which is traceable to such relationships be overestimated; nor is the end in sight. Until some basic agreements can be reached in regard to the rights and obligations of landlords and tenants, landed and landless, the continued development of conflict situations must be expected.

Sharecropping systems of various types are probably the most common forms of tenancy practiced in Peru. Sharecroppers are known by such names as *aparceros, compañeros, medieros, colonos,* or others, depending on the locale. The common feature of all forms of sharecropping is that the tenant pays a given proportion of the crop as rent rather than, as in the case of the standing tenant, a fixed amount. The usual division is by halves, but other proportions may be agreed upon. Customarily the Peruvian proprietor supplies the land and assumes the irrigation costs, if any. He may also supply, depending upon local custom, all, half, or some other fraction of the cost of seed, fertilizer, and tools. The sharecropper supplies all the labor of cultivation and harvest, and the costs that go with them, plus his share of the seed, fertilizer, and equipment. In addition, he is usually expected to maintain the roads of the farm, keep the irrigation ditches clean, and perform such other duties as are necessary to the upkeep of the land which he cultivates. Following the harvest (at which time the proprietor visits the farm, if at no other) the crop is divided according to the agreed proportions. Any loans which the proprietor may have advanced to the tenant, as he frequently has, are paid from the tenant's share of the crop, together with interest. Other customary stipulations of this form of agreement are that there can be no sublease or cession of the contract without the permission of the owner, and that the contract is automatically broken upon the death of the tenant.

Under the sharecropping system the proprietor bears a more equitable share of the risk than is the case when a fixed amount of the crop must be paid by the tenant. Perhaps for this reason the arrangement is much more frequently used for the production of food than for commercial crops. It is a common complaint of proprietors, especially absentee owners, that their share tenants are prone to consume or sell part of the produce before the "official" harvest. On the basis of his own observations, the author is inclined to substantiate this claim. On the other hand, further observations led to the conclusion that such behavior, especially on the part of Indian tenants, is tolerated within limits by the landlords as being normal and expected. Again, one is reminded of the attitudes of Southern white landlords toward the "toting" habits and other peccadilloes of Negro tenants and laborers, actions which are accepted with half-amused forbearance as prima facie evidence of innate inferiority.

In the sierra various forms of share arrangements are employed in livestock production. A common practice is for the tenant to receive one-half the increase of the proprietor's stock in return for his services. Another form is one in which the tenant owns the producing livestock and pays for pasturage rights with a share of the increase. Livestock production sharing seems, from all reports, to be highly conducive to defraudation attempts on the part of both tenants and proprietors. When the livestock belongs to the landlord, herdsmen are held accountable for its welfare, and it is not unknown for them to be forced to pay for alleged but unproved losses (falla).[10] Indians who rent pasture rights under the share system occasionally have their animals corralled with those of the landlord in the annual roundup. In such cases the return of the animals is almost entirely dependent upon the volition of the landowners.[11] Rustling (abigeato) and withholding part of the annual increase are frequently attributed to herdsmen.

The Indians of the sierra practice a form of share production which is called huaqui (or waqui) in some regions and pullan-pura in others, with probably other local names. The system is described by M. Julio Delgado as follows:

The Indian institution called waqui is an alliance of capital and labor. It has two forms, agricultural production and livestock production. In the first the proprietor supplies the land, while his associate supplies the labor and bears related expenses. The cost of the seed is borne by the member providing the land, while the cost of harvesting is shared. The division of the harvest is in equal parts. Waqui is practiced not only among the Indians, but also with a patrón or farm owner.

Livestock waqui is effected through one associate supplying as capital a mother animal—cow, sheep, llama, pacocha, pig or chicken— while the other feeds and otherwise cares for the animals until the young are separable from the mother. The division of the young or the profit from their sale is by halves. If there is only one offspring [per season] the first customarily belongs to the owner of the mother, the next to the one who provides food and care.[12]

Farm Laborers

The consideration of farm laborers as a tenure status group is probably open to some question, inasmuch as they have no defined rights to the land which they work. Nor, for that matter, is their income dependent upon the crop yield, since they are paid for their efforts regardless of whether they are ultimately productive. The justification which must be offered for this apparently illogical inclusion of laborers as a tenure type lies in the fact that in Peru the granting of restricted rights to a portion of land is one of the most common methods of securing farm labor.

The type of wage hand so common in North American agriculture was virtually unknown in Peru before the appearance of a truly commercial agriculture on the coast. This form of agricultural employee is still mostly to be found engaged in such large-scale operations as are afforded by the commercial sugar enterprises, which found the traditional systems of employment unsuitable to their needs. By and large, the wage hand represents a recent cultural innovation by foreign interests accustomed to the relative efficiency of paying laborers fixed amounts of cash for a day's work.

The adaptation of native workers to the alien cash wage system has not been an easy matter, nor has it been completely accomplished as yet. The average sierra Indian or mestizo, reared in an agrarian culture, looks to land of his own cultivation for security. Working as a wage hand offers no hope for the realization of this ambition. Land of his own is something tangible; more than a mere source of income, it offers a home, an intrinsic wealth confirmed by the folklore of countless generations. Money is a transient thing to his mind—welcome, but of limited utility. A new hat, a shirt, some coca and *chicha,* and the month's wages are gone. The future can be viewed only in terms of a succession of gettings and spendings, with never a place to call one's own, whether one really owns it or not.

It is not difficult to understand the sierra Indian's reluctance to leave his mountain home. He faces the cheerless prospect of working with others uprooted like himself, for strangers to whom he is only a name and a number, in a climate where he is likely to contract pulmonary disease. This reluctance of his to accept work opportunities of the coast led to the development of a system of recruitment known as *enganche*. The *enganche* is simply a collective contract of workers for a fixed task. Generally it is arranged through an intermediary known as the *enganchador* or *contratista,* although some haciendas maintain their own recruiting officers in the sierra villages. The *enganchador* is paid a commission for every laborer he recruits. As the system formerly operated, he generally advanced high-interest loans to prospective workers as assurance that they would fulfill the contract. Not infrequently the loans were so large that the workers were unable to repay them with interest during a single contract period and were forced to remain for one or more extra periods in a state of peonage. Until prohibited in 1909, it was a common practice for local political officers to serve as *enganchadores,* exerting their power and prestige to recruit all whom they could. The hope always held out was that of a short period on the coast with high wages, allowing the laborer to return to his mountain community.

Enganche is still practiced today, but mostly for supplying workers for the coca haciendas in the selva. Generally the recruits will contract to work for a part of the year and return to their own lands for planting and harvesting seasons. There is a large seasonal flow of migratory laborers from the sierra to the selva and coast, but no comprehensive studies of the extent and nature of the movement have been made yet. Not all migratory laborers have land ties. Some are unattached and live entirely by the jobs which they can obtain as farm laborers. Positions as tenants are considered more desirable, however, and are relatively easy to obtain if a worker exhibits any merit. As a result, permanent migratory laborers are a small minority element.

In keeping with long-standing tradition, few haciendas pay their laborers entirely in cash, and even the highly commercialized corporate farms have adopted the practice of paying a portion of the wages in rations. It is customary for the smaller farms to supply their workers with food and one or more popular items such as coca, tobacco, or beverage alcohol, the selection being agreed upon by the laborers and patrons. The large sugar estates supply certain basic food rations to their workers as part of their wage and allow them to purchase additional supplies at reduced rates from the company commissaries. Medical attention, hospitalization, and schooling are also available on these larger enterprises, and the housing facilities are generally better than are to be found on smaller haciendas. Such concessions made to the workers do not represent altruism so much as they do the necessity for offering special attractions to recruit and hold labor.

The wages paid to farm laborers are generally quite low, even by Peruvian standards. A study of wages in thirty-six agricultural valleys made by the Ministerio de Agricultura in 1949 revealed that the daily rate varied from 2.50 *soles* (approximately 15 cents, U. S.) with meals to 8.00 *soles* (approximately 48 cents, U.S.) without meals.[13] Wages of skilled laborers, particularly operators of farm machinery, ranged much higher than those of the unskilled wage hands. Since most of the data of the study were taken from coastal valleys, where the pay is higher than in the rest of the country, the average wage of nearly 6.00 *soles* which was recorded is hardly representative of the national situation. In the sierra as late as 1950 wages were sometimes less than one *sol* per day. Customarily men received higher pay than women engaged in comparable tasks. Such a wage scale in itself is sufficient to explain the low purchasing power of the rural proletariat. It should be added that the average worker is seldom able or willing to work every day. He loses many days through illness, and several through travel if his work is far from his home. Then, he must spend some time cultivating his own plot; and there are the frequent religious holidays, all of which subtract from his meager cash income. It is a rare laborer in the sierra whose cash earnings for a year exceed $75; the income of the majority probably falls within the range from $25 to $50 per year.

The traditional system for paying agricultural labor, of course, is not in wages but in land usufruct. This method was inaugurated during the colonial period and has continued to the present time. The main change which has taken place is that formerly the use of the land was the only remuneration which the laborer received, while he is now generally accorded at least a token supplementary cash wage. As late as 1949, though, the director of a government demonstration farm in the sierra province of Puno wrote: "There still persists on some haciendas, as a vestige of the colonial period, the fixed Indian laborer in a condition of material and moral obligation that binds him to the *hacendado;* owing to the fact that he has no other place where he can live, he seeks the shelter of the hacienda and there lends his services almost gratuitously."[14]

The *colonos,* as such serfs are generally called, are undoubtedly the lowest class of agricultural workers in the country, receiving infinitesimal wages for working their required number of days on the hacienda. Nor is their labor the only obligation. Some *hacendados* are known to require their *colonos* to use their own animals in transporting farm produce, without compensation for such service. On other haciendas the wife and children of the *colono* are expected to serve as household servants (*mitañas*), for which they receive little or no remuneration. These demands are not resisted by the *colonos,* except in cases of extreme flagrancy; rather, they tend to be passively accepted as part of the system.

The reasons for the development and preservation of the *colono* system in the sierra are basically the same as those for the system of *yanaconaje* on the coast: the relative scarcity of good farm land; the general lack of working capital; and the complementary attitudes of the white landowners and Indian laborers toward the land and toward each other. The development of commercialized farming on the coast has tended to improve the condition of the *yanacona,* but that of the *colono* has remained relatively static. Only in a few instances can signs of a status change for the latter be detected, and those are subtle. One such example of mobility appears to exist in the development of the tenure status of the *arrendire,* a half-laborer, half-renter. This type of arrangement, which is especially prevalent in the province of Concepción in the department of Cuzco, provides that the *arrendire* shall pay a fixed rent for the land and, in addition, provide specified services to the proprietor. Unlike that of the *colono,* his contract, either verbal or written, is for a fixed period of time, and he is allowed free disposal of his crop.[15] This particular development in an area where rural dwellers are known to be migrating urbanward suggests that *colonos* are being elevated to the status of renters, provided they are still willing to furnish the services necessary to the operation of the unleased portion of the hacienda. A second example of transition is recorded in a significant passage from an unpublished study made by SCIPA (pronounced see' pa) agents in the northern sierra department of Cajamarca. The passage reads: "In the province of Bambamarca, through an agreement between the *hacendados* and the renters, the latter pay a relatively low rent, but must work from ten to fifteen days for the hacienda without receiving any daily wage. Because of the low productivity of the work of these laborers, some *hacendados* prefer that the *colonos* pay them S/15.00 monthly, thus freeing themselves from the work requirement."[16] It seems clear that the *colonos* in the region must originally have been allowed a plot of farm land, *not* for the rent which the proprietors expected to receive, but rather for the labor which they were required to expend on the hacienda. As this labor became unnecessary or uneconomical, or both, the *colonos* were converted into the equivalent of cash renters.

Most *colonos* in the sierra receive at the present time a small cash wage in addition to the use of the land. Legally, a minimum wage of at least twenty centavos per day has been required since 1916, but this sum is so small that it is merely a gesture. In general, the wages of *colonos* are above this minimum, but considerably less than what wagehands with no land attachments receive. The *hacendado,* in addition to the land and wage, also supplies—in conformance with tradition—alcohol and coca for the workers when there are special operations such as the harvest. In some instances he may even provide a food ration. Many different combinations of cash, rations, and land use have been developed as payment for farm labor. Local customs are important determinants of which combination shall be used.

The discussion of farm labor in Peru cannot be concluded without some further mention of family workers, a class including nearly one-fifth of the entire agricultural group, according to the 1940 census. Since rural families are large and incomes are limited, Peruvian farm children must begin to bear their own economic loads at tender ages. This economic necessity has retarded formal education in all rural areas, even those having access to schools. Where the luxury of school-ing can be afforded, it is generally reserved for males, on the good assumption that their income-producing potentialities are greater than those of females. The daughters of rural families, when scarcely out of infancy themselves, are charged with the care of smaller children in order that their mothers can be freed to supplement the family income through working as laborers. Whether from choice or necessity, the family of rural Peru remains the basic economic unit, and all the members must contribute to its operation as soon and as long as they are able.

INDIAN COMUNEROS

Most of the Indian communities in existence today are probably descended from the *reducciones* established during the colonial admin-istration of the viceroy Toledo. Some, however, appear to have been *ayllus* that persisted on the holdings of some Spanish overlord until they finally received land grants of their own. In either case, the communities retain vestiges of pre-Hispanic land practices, although modifications have been so great that it would be a distortion of fact to say that they represent the preservation of the Inca agricultural com-munity.

It has been observed in an earlier chapter that repeated attempts were made during both the colonial and republican eras to eradicate the communal system before the remaining communities were finally accorded recognition as legal entities in 1920. Since then the Peruvian government has exhibited considerably more interest in and concern for their existence. In 1950 more than 1,500 Indian communities were officially registered by the Bureau of Indian Affairs, with a population in excess of one million. This undoubtedly does not represent a com-plete registration, since the census of 1940 classified more than 4,600 populated centers as *comunidades*.[17] Few of these communities actually continue a communal system of land ownership, but the fact that they remain as the last strongholds of the indigenous culture lends signifi-cance to their tenure practices.

It cannot be said that there is any generalized pattern of man-land relationships in the Indian communities, since practices and characteristics vary widely from region to region. The classical system of the *ayllu,* it has been noted, was one under which the community as a whole owned the land, with plots being assigned to various families for cultivation. In many communities the association of particular families with particular plots became so firmly fixed that the system operated for most purposes like that of private ownership. Since this development appears to have taken place prior to our earliest records on the subject, it is difficult to say whether or not it represented any radical evolution from an earlier system. The system of *reducciones* was a synthesis of the *ayllu* and the Spanish village, retaining some of the communal features of both, such as the common pasture. This particular characteristic seems to have disappeared almost entirely from the current scene.

The present-day community, in general, fails to maintain any equality of land distribution among its members or families. Some of the *comuneros* have relatively large holdings, while others are virtually landless, this inequality resulting largely from the operation of the Spanish system of inheritance. Instead of lands being reassigned on the basis of family size, as they once were, they pass through inheritance to offspring. The resulting inequality of distribution has probably contributed as much as anything to the development of tenancy within the communities themselves.

Even though redistribution of the land is no longer practiced, the ritual of land assignment has been retained in many communities. The cultivated lands of the community are frequently divided into sections, called *suertes,* of varying quality. The holdings of a family are generally dispersed among several *suertes,* some of which are cultivated while others lie fallow. The rotation of *suertes* in many communities is formally determined each year by local officials, who designate which ones shall be cultivated. Community sanctions are generally strong enough that the official decision is followed by the *comuneros,* even though it may not be legally binding.

Another vestige of the *ayllu* is the exchange of labor which is widely practiced; this is known as *aine,* as *minga,* and by other local names.[18] *Aine* usually refers to any lending of a personal service in expectation that it will be reciprocated in services of equal order. *Minga* denotes a mass lending of services, either to aid an individual or to accomplish some project of benefit to the entire community.[19] In the latter case, of course, no reciprocation is expected, but considerable community pressure is brought to bear to equalize the burden through requiring the participation of all able-bodied *comuneros. Minga* in agricultural tasks is simply the cooperative work of a number of *comuneros* for the benefit of one of the members. Those who participate are not paid for their labors, but the task is generally carried out in a spirit of festivity, with food, alcohol, and tobacco or coca being supplied to all by the beneficiary of the labor. The receiver, in turn, is obligated to serve any of the participants in the same capacity under equivalent conditions. This system of mutual aid is very similar to that practiced in the house-raisings and husking bees of the North American frontier. In fact, the *minga* is utilized for the accomplishment of both those tasks as well as for many others. A particularly important employment of it is in the holding of religious festivals, with various members cooperating to provide the necessary food, drink, candles, fireworks, and religious decorations. This is frequently done even when one of the members is held solely responsible for the costs of the fiesta, since the other members know that the lot will eventually fall to them. In this sense, the *minga* serves as a mutual loan instrument which allows the *mayordomo* of the fiesta to pay off his incurred debt over a period of months or even years.

In many communities the fiction of communal ownership has been completely discarded and the individual members have legal, private ownership of the lands. Even in these cases, though, mutual aid practices may persist and with them a strong bond of unity among the members. Under such conditions community sanctions against the sale of lands to persons other than community members, particularly whites, can be and are successfully enforced.[20] Yet the fact that private ownership is recognized as a legal right distinguishes these "nominal" communities from the more traditional type.[21]

Even in those communities where the land is theoretically communal, community members may own land privately. This frequently is the case when property adjoining the community lands is offered for sale and can be purchased by *comuneros*. Such lands are then considered to be within the community bounds and differ from the other lands only in that the owners have individual deeds to them.

In the past, communities have frequently lost their lands to encroaching *hacendados* who have taken full legal advantage of hazy boundaries and lack of proper deeds to community lands. As the *comuneros* have learned the significance of the technicalities, they have offered stronger resistance to attempts to defraud them, by hiring lawyers. In a great number of instances, however, the lawyers themselves have taken advantage of their knowledge of legal claims to join in the general extortion. But protection afforded by the national government has gradually strengthened the position of the communities against outsiders. The newly acquired sophistication in the ways of the law has not been an unmixed blessing, however, for now *comuneros* are quick to take their land disputes with other members to the courts. This process not only frequently costs more than the land involved is worth but also furthers the breakdown of community bonds.

In summary, the present tenure pattern—or better, patterns—represents the incomplete synthesis of two distinct systems with new factors being added during the mixing process. The fact that the two cultures represented came into contact through conquest has served to color all subsequent relationships. It largely explains why the European system of private ownership has almost completely supplanted the native system of collective ownership, and it certainly explains why the Indians have held a virtual monopoly of the least favorable tenure positions.

The Spanish talent for exploitation was restricted to the human realm and did not extend to the land. Peru would have been a rather barren conquest had the conquerors not been able to secure the labor of the native element in the mines and the fields. And the fact must be noted that the subjects of the Inca submitted much more readily than did the conquered natives in other parts of the New World. It is hard not to believe that their previous subjugation had facilitated their exploitation by the Spaniards, that their love of the land meant more than did their own freedom. It is one of the strange contradictions of the colonial period that the crown in trying to give them freedom led them deeper into bondage. The same held true for the early republic, whose leaders could not understand the perils of unaccustomed liberty.

It is easy to condemn the white landowners for their avarice and cruelty, but this does not shed any light on the true relationship that existed, or exists. It is doubtful that the landowners thought of themselves as exploiters of the native element. More likely they felt that they were exhibiting kindness toward the Indians by allowing them to live on the land without paying any cash rent. For that matter, it is also doubtful that many of the Indians thought of themselves as being particularly exploited, for it will be remembered that under the Incas they had been expected to cultivate the fields of the Inca and the Sun as well as their own plots. Quite probably they had more real freedom on some of the haciendas than their forefathers had experienced under Inca domination. Certainly the flights from Toledo's *reducciones* to private haciendas indicate that many of them felt better treatment could be obtained from the private landowners.

Perhaps one clue to the cooperation of the Indians lies in the prevalence of absentee ownership during the colonial period and the republic. As long as the landlord was more interested in owning the land than he was in making it productive, the demands on native labor were not likely to be too heavy. Generally the administration of agricultural operations was left to some responsible mestizo who served as the *mayordomo*. The strictness of his control was determined by the demands of the *patrón* and by his own character. Some were undoubtedly cruel to their charges; but such instances were more likely to be recorded than those to the contrary. Usually the *mayordomo* knew little more about cultivation techniques than did the laborers, so cultivation practices underwent no radical alterations as a result of Spanish influence, with the possible exception of the introduction of the plow.

The development of large-scale commercial agriculture on the coast, beginning in the middle of the nineteenth century, set into motion a series of changes in the tenure system of that region. Because the coastal valleys were exceptionally fertile and accessible the Indians had been almost completely dislodged from them by that time. It was difficult to lure Indians down from the sierra, so Negro slavery was tried, without great success, until its abolition in 1855. Even though landowners frequently took every advantage of their economic position, the status of *yanaconas* was still clearly superior to that of an attached laborer. Furthermore, as the demand for skilled agricultural labor increased, the status of the *yanaconas* rose even higher, as did the statuses of other types of tenants.

The system of *yanaconaje* was not suitable to the operations of the larger sugar estates, nor was it necessary there, since the owners generally possessed greater investment capital than did the individual hacienda owners. Therefore they introduced the system of cash hands, not only because it was better suited to their mass production methods but also because many of the administrators were foreigners who were unaccustomed to the more cumbersome system of granting tillage rights in exchange for labor. However, even they have not been able to escape completely the dictates of tradition and have found it expedient to continue the expected perquisites of food rations and other provisions.

In the sierra commercial agriculture is still in its embryonic stages, and status gains of tenants are less noticeable although not completely undetectable. Indirectly they have benefited through legislation which responded to the growing power of agricultural labor on the coast. Few, if any, of the measures passed have ever been enforced, but landowners have nevertheless made concessions to labor demands even while denying their validity. Thus, the *colonos* of the sierra are now paid a cash wage in addition to being allowed the use of some land, but they still reman the lowest of all tenants and laborers.

In the Indian communities there have also been significant changes in recent times. The tardy recognition of the collective ownership rights of the communities has meant that such rights are seldom exercised any more. Private ownership is the general practice, either legally or virtually, and with it have come unequal distribution of the land, and tenancy. Having curbed the land encroachments of outsiders to a great extent, the *comuneros* reveal considerable internal dissension over land rights and uses.

The problems of rural Peru are largely the problems of its Indian population, and the economic future of Peru is largely dependent upon their solution. If the indigenous population can be successfully absorbed into an urban industrial system, the transition may be relatively peaceful. But there are many factors which impede such a process, no few of which are to be found in the structure and condition of Indian society itself. Since these are matters of such fundamental importance, they have been accorded a more detailed treatment in the following chapter.

5.

The Indian in the Peruvian Agrarian Scheme

THE INDIAN PROBLEMS OF PERU are not abso-
lutely identical with the agrarian problems of the nation, but the area
of common ground probably comprises the greater portion of both sets
of problems. Anyone who begins an analysis of the factors involved
in one set soon finds that he is also dealing with the other. To judge
from the literature, it would appear that most such studies have started
with Indians rather than agrarian difficulties, and the number of them
that have been made is astounding. Moisés Sáenz, the Mexican social
scientist, noted this phenomenon when he wrote: "There is probably
no other country in America where the preoccupation with the Indian,
or at least with Indian questions, is more profound or more widespread
than in Peru. The bibliographic movement reveals this restlessness;
historians, sociologists, jurists, writers—for the past twenty years all
have been concerned with the Indian."[1]

To study the Indian in Peru means to study rural life and agriculture. "The rural life worker *is* the Indian," Luis Valcárcel once
noted. "The day he should disappear, agriculture [in Peru] would
suffer a death blow."[2] Valcárcel's statement is probably not so true
today, at least on the coast, as it was when he made it. Nevertheless,
one might as well attempt to understand race relations in Mississippi
without considering cotton and the plantation system as to deal with the
Peruvian Indian and his problems while disregarding the agrarian
economy and his role in it. The peculiar thing is that the linkage
between Indian problems and agrarian problems is so close that its
significance tends to be overlooked, except when periodic rediscoveries

103

of the relationship are made. The precursor of left-wing politics in Peru—González Prada—highlighted the association when he argued in 1924, "The Indian question, more than pedagogical, is economic, is social."[3] This opinion found ready reiteration in the works of the brilliant and influential Marxist José Carlos Mariátegui. In his famous *7 Ensayos de Interpretación de la Realidad peruana*, Mariátegui further elaborated upon the theme: "The Indian question stems from our economy. It has its roots in the system of land ownership."[4] After his death, though, Mariátegui's many disciples were willing to let the matter stand where the master had left it, and what appeared to be a promising beginning degenerated into a banal conclusion.

Upon more thorough investigation, it can be seen that the nexus between the related sets of Indian and agrarian problems is much more complex than the oversimplified Marxian postulate expounded by Mariátegui. It is undeniable, of course, that the system of land distribution did impose a heavy economic burden upon the Indian group, as has been pointed out in the previous chapters. It does not necessarily follow, though, that all their difficulties are bound up in this one fact.

There is considerable reason to suppose that the Indian culture of Peru would have faced serious problems of adjustment following contact with European culture, even if the Spanish had accorded the population generous treatment and allowed the natives to retain their agricultural lands. The Inca system was rigid, relatively static, and in most respects out of harmony with European cultural patterns. Considering the aims of the Spanish, it is difficult to see how conflict could have been avoided. But there is little to be gained from speculation as to what might have happened had the Spanish not come as conquerors, or had they not come at all. The reality is that they did come and that they dominated the native peoples through force, superimposing various aspects of their culture upon that of the Indians and disrupting completely an elaborate political and economic system. Since this upheaval no comparable equilibrium of social and economic forces has been achieved.

Another item that must be considered in attempting to understand the Indian's role is the fact that the indigenous culture has been considered inferior to that of the whites. Mouth honor has certainly been accorded various aspects of the native culture, but from a practical standpoint it is to be recognized that the flow of acculturation has been predominantly from the conquerors to the conquered, from white to Indian. To a considerable extent mestizo culture does blend the traits of both. Nevertheless, the *cholo* who rises to a position of social eminence does so through discarding his Indian habits and adopting almost exclusively the European way of life. The aspiring leader may find it politically expedient to call himself a *cholo,* but he is not likely to find himself accepted by the genteel society of Lima if he behaves like one.

To speak of *the* Indian or of *the* Indian problem in Peru is misleading to a certain extent, suggesting a homogeneity that does not actually exist. There are, of course, a number of different indigenous groups in the highlands, the two basic cultures being the Quechua and the Aymara. Apart from initial variances, there has been a differential dispersion of European culture as a result of differences in location and accessibility of the various groups. The Indian population, therefore, is far from a unified group, either culturally or socially. Yet, though we recognize this fact, the treatment of this ethnic element as a functional whole in certain considerations is not completely unwarranted. So far as the man-land relational systems of Peru are concerned, it is to be recognized that the Indians are an agricultural people, that they are stereotyped in the mind of the white society, and—of greatest significance—that they are relegated to a subordinate position. Whatever their fundamental differences may be in actuality, they are equated in terms of social and economic discrimination.

The 1940 census enumerated an Indian population of more than three million in Peru. Since the classification was made on a racial basis, it might be speculated that a cultural definition of Indians would include many thousands more who were classified by the census as mestizos. Of the entire Indian population, it may be conservatively estimated that 70 to 75 per cent are engaged in or directly dependent upon agriculture or animal husbandry enterprises for their livelihood.[5] This being true, Indians compose the bulk of Peruvian rural society.

The full significance of this rests on the fact that the economy of Peru is still largely an agrarian economy, dependent for its prosperity upon the activities and welfare of the farm group.

Even though it comprises the majority element of the rural population, the Indian group, as we have seen, makes a relatively small contribution in terms of commercial productivity. The explanation for this lies in the interrelationship of factors which have been previously noted: the scarcity of good land, primitive agricultural techniques, and the fact that the social structure is geared to a subsistence rather than a market economy. It is practically impossible for most of the Indian farmers to produce a surplus, considering the conditions under which they must operate. In the sierra the Indian still prepares his small plot of land with the *chaquitaclla,* a digging stick antedating the plow, improved in the past 400 years only through the addition of an iron point. He can afford no other implements, and, even if he could, the terrain is frequently too rugged to allow their use. He lives in a windowless adobe house of one or two rooms, lacking even the most rudimentary furniture, which serves to shelter his animals as well as his family. The energy at his disposal is almost entirely supplied by human muscle. He customarily carries heavy loads on his back, suspended by a rope that passes over his shoulders and is knotted on his chest. His wife makes thread on a hand spindle, and weaves on a hand loom, utilizing patterns of centuries past.

Admittedly, much of what today is defined as the Indian problem is simply anachronistic behavior. The sixteenth-century living conditions of the Indian are judged to be bad by twentieth-century standards which are not his own; his economic operations appear inefficient and time-consuming only when contrasted with the productivity of a more advanced technology than he possesses or may even care to possess. But, whether he wants to or not, the Indian cannot live in an isolated world; he is being forced to compete for survival in a larger sphere in which his own conditions of life place him at a disadvantage. He is not going to be left undisturbed and Peru can no longer afford to let him merely subsist.

The unpreparedness of the Indian population to participate in contemporary culture is clearly revealed by the census data on literacy. Illiteracy was no problem to the Inca administration, or even during the colonial or early republican eras, because it was no bar to successful functioning in those societies. Today literacy is a virtual necessity, because so much communication is through the medium of the printed word. Yet in the six sierra departments with the highest proportions of Indian population, 72 to 88 per cent of the persons fifteen years of age and over had in 1940 received no formal education.[6] Of the group of children in the six- through fourteen-year bracket, 80 to 88 per cent had never attended school.[7] It does not seem an unwarranted conclusion that the Indian population as represented in these departments is at a disadvantage for functioning in the civilization by whose standards it is judged. Nor can it be argued any longer that they will not have to function in such a civilization. The population growth, the limited land supply, the already swelling flow of urbanward migration offer ample refutation. It is not a question of whether they will participate, but of how.

Another indication of the general state of Peruvian Indian life is to be found in the health conditions of the group. Dr. Maxime Kuczynski Godard has published a series of monographs based on field investigations in Indian communities, revealing the findings of admittedly cursory physical examinations. Even without elaborate diagnostic techniques, the physician found high incidences of intestinal parasitic disorders, cataracts and other eye diseases, pellagra, hyperthyroidism evidenced by goiter, hypothyroidism evidenced by cretinism, deaf-mutes, skin eruptions, pyorrhea, dental caries, and numerous other diseases stemming from dietary deficiency.[8] Such findings would suggest that many of the Indians are not able to maintain themselves at even a subsistence level. The maladies of Peru responsible for the greatest number of fatalities are pneumonia and influenza, whooping cough, enteritis, childhood diseases, avitaminosis, and malaria.[9] All these are preventable or controllable when modern hygienic practices and medical techniques are applied. But the Indian has no such equipment; his knowledge of basic sanitation and hygiene is virtually nil. Disease is treated in accordance with the prescriptions of folklore and superstition. Even when physicians are available, which is seldom the case, the Indians are more likely to resort to the native *brujo* for treatment with herbs and magic incantations.

It is significant, although not surprising, that such a high proportion of physical maladies encountered among the Indians is related to diet, for undernourishment is a normal accompaniment of low social and economic status. The general inadequacy of the Indian's diet, which is to be inferred from a study of his diseases, has been directly revealed in the studies of food consumption made by SCIPA. To cite one of these, in 1946-1947 an investigation was made of the dietary habits of one thousand Indian and mestizo families residing in over 100 rural communities. It was found that the value of food consumed by 90 per cent of the families was less than one *sol* per person per day. This sum, less than six cents of the United States dollar at the free exchange rate of the period, included the estimated values of home-produced foods as well as those small quantities that were purchased. Of course, the important matter is not the cost of the food but the content. In practically no case, according to the cited study, was the caloric content of the meals adequate to the needs of the consumers, being deficient in some instances by as much as 50 per cent. Some of this deficiency was the natural result of an insufficient quantity of food, but most of it was traceable to an unbalanced diet. Fresh vegetables, citrus fruits, butter, and fats were notably lacking; milk and cheese were practically never consumed. Other readily available foods that could have supplied needed vitamins and calories were disdained mainly because of cultural traditions relative to food. The conclusions of the study are important because they point out the connection between man-land relationships, income, and health. They read, in part:

. . . The causes of nutritional deficiency in the zones studied are of three orders: poverty, ignorance, and poor budgeting of the rent or salary.

The families of the agricultural zones are, in the majority, poor, small landowners; and, because the lands are subdivided, the farmers possess a limited amount of cultivable land to serve as the source of subsistence—to supply clothing, habitation, and luxury items as well as the food necessities. The dwelling generally is in keeping, with no provisions for either hygiene or comfort.

The economic situation of the small farmer who is not a proprietor is worse, because if he is a peon or day laborer, his salary is so low that it does not pay for his eating every day; he lives in constant indebtedness to the *tambos* where he buys his food, paying a high commission. If he cultivates rented land, he operates as a *yanacona, compañero, arrendatario, partidario,* etc. All these systems are disadvantageous to the small farmer, because what he raises does not yield enough to cover both the rent of the land and the subsistence necessities.[10]

In discussing the dietary habits and health of the Peruvian Indians the use of coca should not be omitted. Many investigators have pointed out the relationship between the widespread Indian custom of chewing coca leaves and the dietary deficiency of the group. It is difficult to say whether the use of coca is a cause or result of inadequate food consumption, but the cocaine content of the leaves is sufficient to repress normal hunger drives. If the leaves are chewed in large quantities and with sufficient frequency, cocaine addiction may result; however, the proportion of such addicts to the number of users is relatively small. Whatever may be its physical effects, the use of coca imposes a great economic burden upon the Indian population, costing more than a million dollars annually.[11] The recorded consumption of coca in 1946 was 7,415,239 kilograms, a figure that represented a 50 per cent increase in consumption over a ten-year period. Quite plausibly the most deleterious effect of coca upon the Indian diet may not be the direct effect upon his digestive system but the siphoning off of money that might otherwise be spent for food.

To summarize the general life conditions of the contemporary Peruvian Indian, he farms a small portion of land with primitive techniques yielding him and his family a food supply that is barely adequate in quantity and generally inadequate in nutritive content. As a consequence, rural Indians are not healthy but suffer from a variety of maladies stemming from poor diet, and are also the victims of numerous other diseases simply because of ignorance of the most elementary principles of preventive medicine. Nor is their ignorance limited to matters of diet and health. They are generally unprepared to participate in any social and cultural system except that under which they are so poorly faring. Yet it is upon the labor of this group, impoverished, undernourished, and afflicted, that so much of the important agricultural economy of the nation is based.

It might be justly asked why the basic position of the Indian population has remained so little altered during the four centuries since contact was first made with representatives of European culture and society. The most plausible explanations for this, it is suggested, may be grouped under three broad headings: (1) the attitudes and actions of the non-Indian society; (2) the static nature of the Indian culture itself; and (3) the Indian personality.

Considering the first of these, it is an irrefutable fact that the Peruvian Indian has met with discrimination and exploitation at the hands of the non-Indian segment of the population, and in particular the white element. There are those who claim that racial prejudice does not exist in Peru, offering as evidence the considerable racial intermixture that has taken place and the high social and political status that has been gained by some mestizos. This is begging the question, however, and is a valid argument only on the technical grounds of the constitution of biological race: as such, it ignores the fact that social and economic discrimination can be directed against minorities other than the purely racial. Cultural differences, as Peru clearly demonstrates, may serve an equally invidious function.

The origins of the traditional Spanish-Indian relationships were outlined in an earlier chapter, these being the *encomienda* system, the expropriation of Indian agricultural lands, and the imposition of forced labor and tribute. Despite the diluting effects of the intervening decades, the attitudes of both conqueror and conquered engendered during the early colonial era have drifted down to the present. This is no mere persistence of ancient prejudices; the current relationship stems more from the fact that the Indians were never able to recover from the inferior social and economic position in which they were placed as a result of the conquest. In the eyes of some, the subordinate position itself appeared to offer justification for further exploitation, if such treatment required justification, on the grounds that low status demonstrated innate inferiority. Peru, of course, was not the only country in the New World in which robbing and cheating the natives became a leading business enterprise and a national pastime.

Gamonalismo was the descriptive Spanish term applied to the system of Indian exploitation in Peru. Of the connotations of the word Moisés Sáenz wrote:

Gamonalismo is an order of things, a social state, an attitude: it means the condition of inequality of the Indian with respect to the other social classes of the country, the extrasocial conditions of which Mariátegui spoke; it is colonialism and clericalism projected through a century of independent life; it signifies spoliation, neofeudalism; it means the connivance of the social classes of authorities, clergy, and landholders in exploiting the Indians without conscience and without scruple.[12]

The "connivance" of which Sáenz wrote is more rare today than it once was. *Gamonalismo* has fallen into general disrepute, although it has by no means completely disappeared. More frequently to be observed in the relations of whites and Indians is an attitude of paternalism on the part of the former—the disappearing type of paternalism one may still occasionally see in the treatment of Negro workers by white bosses in the southern United States. The *patrón* of a Peruvian hacienda is likely to exhibit a great deal of personal kindness, to allow indulgences, so long as the work of his Indian laborers and tenants is carried out to his satisfaction. At the same time he will loudly voice his vexation at their slowness, laziness, stupidity, and general inefficiency. His display of injured righteousness in response to the exploitation charges of would-be reformers is not feigned, but quite genuine. He will maintain, often with considerable truth, that far from exploiting his *colonos* (or *yanaconas* or *partidarios*), he allows them to live on the land at a financial loss to himself, since the land could be more profitably farmed under some other system. Like the plantation owner of the Old South, he is puzzled, hurt, and angered at the condemnation of his paternalism, which he regards as Christian charity in the fullest sense.

Although calculated exploitation has declined to a considerable extent in recent decades, it cannot be said that there have been many effective positive actions directed toward the raising of their general social and economic status except those taken by the government. One of the most revealing clues to the conditions of bygone days is the present-day sentiment of many whites that abstention from exploiting the Indians is in itself a grace bestowed. Philip Ainsworth Means once noted this typical attitude of the whites toward the Indians in a description of haciendas in northern Peru. "It is a difficult matter to exaggerate the power for good and likewise for evil which rests in the hands of the landholding portion of the white upper class," he wrote, and continued, "I am prepared to say that the majority of *hacendados* in the Piura-Tumbes region do not abuse their power, but neither do they avail themselves of the almost limitless opportunities for bettering the conditions and brightening the lives of the Indians and mestizos on their estates."[13] There is still little indication that white landowners feel any obligations toward their Indians except the negative one of not mistreating them. So long as such a feeling prevails, it can hardly be expected that the status of the Indian group will be improved by any conscious efforts of the controlling class. Yet the virtual impossibility of any autonomous rise may be seen in the analysis of various aspects of the Indian culture and personality.

It is one thing to attribute the inferior social and economic status of the Indian to white exploitation and quite another to say that the cessation of such exploitation is the remedy to all the ills of the indigenous group. With a few notable exceptions, the response of the Indian population to the aggressive actions of the whites has been one of passive acceptance. This lack of retaliatory action—a source of constant wonder to the conquistadors—suggests that resilience was not a notable quality of the Inca culture, and the reasons for this are fairly apparent. Social organization under the Incas was quite rigid, with sharply drawn class lines. The keynote of the system was cooperation, and there was little opportunity for individual initiative on the part of the common citizenry. The higher education of the ruling classes, who were the only ones that received formal schooling, consisted largely of learning the precepts and following the examples of outstanding antecedents. The guiding principle for the masses was a simple one: obedience to the orders of their superiors. The system established in accordance with this philosophy was orderly and effective, as we have seen, but it was not flexible nor adaptable to changed conditions.

The disorganization of the Inca Empire as a result of the Spanish conquest provided just the type of situation with which the plebeian masses were least equipped to cope. Where they were left relatively undisturbed by the conquerors, they continued in their timeworn grooves of planting, cultivating, harvesting. But the places where such tranquil enterprise persisted were few. Accustomed to receiving and obeying directions, the natives simply took orders from their new rulers, who were considerably more interested in their own welfare than in that of their charges.

The Spanish, for the most part, were content to preserve, and even encouraged, among the native proletariat the traits of servitude and obedience which the Incas had instilled. The main item of the Indian culture which they felt called upon to change was the religion. This was done simply through imposing Roman Catholicism upon the native sects, with an acceptable synthesis being achieved in amazingly short order. Except for the introduction of the plow on the coast and the transfer of European plants to the New World, the Spanish made few contributions to Indian agriculture. They were not interested in providing formal education for the Indians. Few of the whites themselves had received any, and those who had considered it unnecessary for Indians and a potential threat to the maintenance of order. In fact, so long as they did not interfere with the aims of the Spanish the cultural traits and customs of the Indians were not intentionally disturbed to any great extent.

It was inevitable that Indian society and culture should change as a result of association with the Spanish. But there is real significance in the fact that the changes which resulted from contact were not mere adoptions of Spanish culture. The Indians did not readily accept European culture nor, for that matter, did the Europeans desire such acceptance. The whites could retain a superordinate position only so long as the Indians remained subordinate. The Hispanicization of the Indians would have removed the major basis of distinction and spelled the end of their subservience. So long as most of the Indians continued to act

like Indians, it was not necessary to raise social barriers against the relatively few who acted like whites. And the majority of the Indians, as we
have seen, were prepared to continue in their traditional ways when
allowed, and to accept passively their inferior role. Whatever their
antagonisms against the whites, they remained submissive, obeisant.
This being the relationship between the two races, rapid acculturation
was impossible.

The Indian personality, so far as its typical features are concerned,
has reflected the cultural values of the group, the patterned social relations, and the general situations in which the Indian has operated. The
personality product of these factors presents to the average white a
stereotyped yet unfathomable picture. One hears the Indian described
as sullen, lazy, superstitious, dishonest, servile, cowardly, untrusting,
untrustworthy, and lacking in ambition. The notion is widespread that
the Indian affects a deceptively obsequious role in the presence of
whites, and no few read sinister meanings into what they consider a
calculated concealment of unmitigated malice. Those who seek to
fathom this enigmatic behavior frequently end as they began, with what
the Peruvian sociologist Francisco Pastor described as "an infuriating
incomprehension of that race which neither offers its hand nor offers
fight."[14]

As perplexing as it may seem to some, the Indian personality is not
overly difficult to understand when the factors which have produced it
are examined. From the pre-Hispanic culture came his conservatism,
quasi-religious agrarianism, and a compliant response to authority. It
requires no psychoanalysis, either, to understand the resentment toward
the whites who have exploited his race for centuries. If this resentment
is concealed by a façade of timorous servility, it is because the Indian has
been well conditioned not to display his rancor openly, through such
cruel measures as those taken against a few rebellious souls like Tupac
Amaru. There seems nothing peculiar in the fact that the Indian should
not reveal his true attitude toward those whom he dislikes but fears even
more.

The frequently observed surface manifestation of the Indian's
adjustment to his position of social and economic inferiority is an atti-

tude of stolid resignation. More indicative of his true internal state, perhaps, are the evidences of psychological escapism through the immoderate consumption of alcohol and coca. Certainly many of his religious fiestas, which on occasions develop into drunken debauches lasting a week or more, may be interpreted as escape mechanisms.[15] As such, they often provide opportunities for the release of latent hostilities, which, as a point of social psychological interest, are more frequently directed against other Indians than against whites.

There is a widespread belief, at least among the whites, that the Indian or mestizo who is placed in a position of authority is more abusive toward his subordinates than are whites in equivalent positions. The native *caciques* at the head of Indian communities during the colonial and early republican eras reputedly exploited their own race with greater cruelty than did any other types of administrators. A recent writer discussing the relative unimportance of racial bonds among hacienda personnel states:

. . . in order not to lose his position, he [the *mayordomo*] must get what he can out of the Indians to demonstrate his ability, his "experience." He is not an intellectual; he is a man of the field who considers the Indian . . . as either an obstacle or an object for rigorous exploitation. Although at times an Indian by "race," he is not so by situation, by social status, and he identifies himself with his master: his aim, his credo, his virtue is to make the Indian work.[16]

It is quite possible that such behavior is also a form of displaced aggression, but, misdirected or not, it has the effect of undermining the establishment of an ethnic solidarity which might serve as a base from which social and economic movements might develop.

It would require a thoroughly circumspect observer to detect among the Peruvian Indians the strong feelings of racial or cultural loyalty which occasionally are attributed to them.[17] And there are logical reasons for doubting their existence. Such identification bonds develop from either widespread communication or a high level of abstraction, neither of which appears to be characteristic of the average rural Indian. The abstract conception of a general "Indian problem," for instance, does not appear to be a product of Indian thought processes; it is the contribution of university intellectuals, for the most part. Limited in his contacts with his fellow sierra dwellers, the Indian is more likely to frame his problems in local terms: the problems of his community, of his family, or, perhaps, of just himself. The current lack of unity and the existence of intraethnic strife is symptomatic of an advanced state of social disorganization which must necessarily retard any general amelioration of the conditions of Indian life. Social mobility, so long as it must be purchased at the expense of exploiting or denying one's own people, will continue to be on an individual rather than a group basis.

The operation of the various factors which have been discussed in the preceding paragraphs is such that the interrelated sets of Indian and agrarian problems tend to perpetuate themselves. One can begin tracing the patterns of causes and consequences at almost any point in the complex web and soon find himself back with his initial consideration. To illustrate, the low socioeconomic status of the Indian farm population has as its consequence a low potential of purchasing power. Low purchasing power retards the development of national industries that would be dependent upon an internal market. The lack of sufficient industrial development to absorb excess rural population perpetuates the conditions of extremely small land divisions among the Indian landholders and the low wages available to farm laborers. These conditions in turn contribute to the reduced agricultural productivity, the inferior socioeconomic position of the Indians, the low purchasing power. The vicious circle—one of many such—is completed.

Almost every measure which has been advanced for the solution of the Indian and agrarian problems premises the breaking of the circle at some point. Education presumes that parents will be able to afford to keep a child in school; the adoption of improved agricultural techniques has as its prerequisites some education and usually some investment capital; industrial expansion premises a market; even the oft-posited panacea of land reform through redistribution of holdings gives no solution unless better cultivation techniques than those currently practiced by the Indians are introduced in conjunction. Disentanglement of the Indian from this web of social, cultural, and economic strands offers no easy task. His own background has not prepared him to do the job himself, and the elements of the white population that are so genuinely desirous of seeing the position of the Indian improved that they are willing to exert some effort in his behalf are still in the minority.

Even so, it cannot be maintained that the situation of the Indian is such that he cannot possibly be extricated. There are already processes under way which carry potentialities of radical alteration of the social and economic structure of Peru. These will be discussed in the following chapter. It must still remain questionable, though, whether such processes can evolve with sufficient rapidity to offset what may be an impending crisis of the current order.

6.

Reform Measures

SOME OF THE MAJOR agrarian problems of Peru have been presented, and it is only natural to ask what measures have been and are being taken to solve them. Whether such measures can be strictly considered "agrarian reform" is difficult to say, since the concept is an ill-defined one and subject to many interpretations. In its more limited sense, agrarian reform connotes a social movement, frequently of a revolutionary type, directed at the alteration of the social and economic conditions of an oppressed agricultural class. As such, it generally embodies a program of land reform directed at changing land distribution, tenure systems, or both. If Mexico be taken as the classic Latin American example of this type of agrarian reform movement, then it can be said that the situation in Peru has remained comparatively unchanged in this regard. On the other hand, if agrarian reform be defined in a broader sense as any measures directed toward improving the conditions of underprivileged agricultural groups, some appreciable efforts have been made in this direction by the Peruvian government.

For that matter, it is not completely satisfactory to restrict the concept to those measures which are specifically aimed at aiding agricultural groups. Farm groups may actually receive greater indirect benefits from the adoption of some general economic policy, for example, than from some legislative enactment in their special behalf. One might ask, also, whether provisions for improving the lot of the Indian could be considered as agrarian reform. Obviously, measures in their behalf affect a major portion of the rural population, but they are neither limited to nor inclusive of the handicapped agricultural group. It would

118

appear that almost any criteria that one chooses for establishing the boundaries of agrarian reform measures are, to a certain extent, of an arbitrary nature. Through exercising this privilege of arbitrary determination two general categories of agrarian reform in Peru may be indicated: sociopolitical movements which have sought sweeping reforms through radical changes in government structure and policy; and general remedial measures offered for the amelioration of various aspects of the over-all problem without radically altering basic political systems and policies.

SOCIOPOLITICAL MOVEMENTS

The Mexican agrarian revolution of 1910 brought, and has continued to bring, predictions of a similar movement in Peru. It has yet to come. The few comparable actions initiated in Peru have seldom proceeded far beyond the ranks of the intellectuals who fomented them. Thus, while there are certain obvious similarities, the existence of substantial differences in the Mexican and Peruvian situations is apparent in the very fact that no agrarian revolution has developed in the latter country.

The first serious attempt to deal with agrarian problems under the republic is to be seen in Bolívar's land reform measures. Whatever ideological effects they may have had, his policies were reduced to mere gestures, so far as their application was concerned, by the recurrent political struggles of the following decades. Social and agricultural reform measures did occasionally appear in the legislation of the nineteenth century, but the general lack of serious attempts to administer them suggests that, for the most part, they were the political sops of successful *caudillos* rather than the work of organized social or political groups.

With the twentieth century there dawned a new type of social consciousness in Peru. Its beginnings may be most clearly seen in the writings of Manuel González Prada, whom Jorge Basadre has called "the founder of Peruvian radicalism."[1] Prada was the voice of a growing sentiment of social unrest. Lashing out in his literary works at what he considered the ills, injustices, and stupidities of his day, he became an effective force more through his later influence than in the actual achievements of his lifetime.[2]

The leading liberal action group in the early twentieth century was the Pro-Indian Association, organized by a group of intellectuals for the purposes of giving gratuitous legal aid to the Indians and sponsoring legislation in their behalf. The Association was in active existence from 1909 to 1917, but its influence, too, extended beyond its own life, as evidenced by the passage of legislation favoring the Indians in the early 1920's. The Constitution of 1920 accorded recognition to the Indian communities as corporate entities, and in 1921 a special bureau for Indian affairs was established in the Ministry of Supply. In 1922 the Patronage of the Indian Race was organized. This was a government agency with the stated functions of protecting the Indians and stimulating their cultural and economic development.[3]

The main line of the liberal intellectual movement set into motion by Prada's agitations continued apart from the Pro-Indian Association and, in general, assumed a Marxist orientation. The chief focus of left-wing thought in the late 1920's was found in the person of José Carlos Mariátegui and the so-called Amauta group of which he was the leader. In the Inca Empire the name "Amauta" had referred to the high functionaries who formulated government policy. Mariátegui chose the name for the influential periodical which he edited and in which many liberal themes were voiced. Unlike Prada, Mariátegui was not content with mere verbalizing and sought the organization of a branch of the Third Communist International in the Peruvian Socialist Party. This attempt was blocked mainly by the Communist Party itself, which would neither accept Mariátegui's interpretation of Marxist doctrine nor subscribe to the maintenance of the Socialist Party guise.[4] As a consequence, the Peruvian radical group split into two factions. After Mariátegui's premature death both sides laid claim to his sanction while continuing their vicious opposition to each other. In the long run, it can be said that Mariátegui's chief influence, like that of Prada, lay in his writings. It was he who lent an agrarian flavor to the developing political movement, stating in his now famous 7 *Ensayos de Interpretación de la Realidad peruana:*

The agrarian problem presents itself, above all, as the problem of the liquidation of feudalism in Peru. . . . The forms of surviving feudalism are two: latifundia and servitude. Related and similar forms whose analysis leads to the conclusion that the servitude which weighs on the Indian race cannot be liquidated without liquidating the latifundia.

Thus posited, the agrarian problem of Peru does not lend itself to mistaken distortions. It appears in all its magnitude as a socioeconomic —and therefore political—problem. And every desire to change it, for example, into a technical agricultural problem within the dominion of agronomists, is a vain endeavor.[5]

The crest of Mariátegui's reform wave broke with his death, but even as it subsided it was overtaken and superseded by a third wave in the rising tide of social protest. Like its antecedents, the new movement originated with and found its support among university students; at the same time it represented a sympathetic and amplified response to the vibrations of González Prada, the guiding spirit of the initial wave. The directing genius of the new action was Victor Raúl Haya de la Torre, who had first gained renown in intellectual circles as the President of the First National Congress of Peruvian Students, which was held in Cuzco in 1920. This congress had itself been a liberal convocation of sorts at which plans were adopted for the establishment of public universities bearing the name of González Prada. Some were actually founded, but proved short-lived. In 1923 Haya headed a student demonstration against the Leguía administration. As a result he was promptly deported; many of his followers met with a harsher fate.[6]

It was during this period of exile that Haya crystallized plans for the movement that was to become the Alianza Popular Revolucionaria Americana (APRA). Conceived as an independent American form of Marxism, the new association offered as its goals the combating of Yankee imperialism, the achievement of Latin American political unity, the nationalization of land and industry, the internationalization of the Canal Zone, and the furtherance of the union of all oppressed classes and peoples of the world.[7] In reality, the international base of the party was not so wide as indicated by its program. The more modest hope, which was still fairly ambitious, was the unification of those American countries possessing large Indian populations.

It was the interpretation of Indo-American problems as unique conditions that split both Mariátegui and Haya de la Torre from conventional Marxism. The Communist Party consistently refused to admit that the Indians differed substantially from any other oppressed proletarian class. Because of his differing views Mariátegui had not been given the support of the Third International, which he felt was necessary to the solution of Peruvian agrarian problems. Haya de la Torre's views were even more heterodox. Although he willingly subscribed to Marxist economic theory, he felt that the Communist Party was not equipped to handle the problems of the Latin-Indian group. "The Communist Party, centralized in Moscow, is the party of the industrial worker," he wrote. "This is a newborn class in the agricultural nations of Latin America. Its problem, that of the Indian, is rooted in agriculture, not in industry. It is, therefore, a unique problem."[8] It is not to be wondered that the Communist Party, which had staged its most successful revolution in preindustrial Russia, was offended by Haya's definition of its proper sphere of operations.

Although not adhering to the Communist Party line, the Aprista Party early adopted Communist tactics and organized party cells in various Latin American countries. In 1931 APRA counted its strength sufficient to support the presidential candidacy of Haya against Sánchez Cerro, who had deposed Leguía. There seems little doubt that Haya was the more popular candidate, but his popularity was no match for the armed might of the dictator. The elections were simply set aside, and Sánchez Cerro retained his power. Then, with brutal directness, he began a bloody extirpation of the Aprista Party that was halted only by his assassination in 1933.

The great popularity gained by APRA in such a relatively short time can be accounted for by the personal appeal of Haya and by the program offered. The nature of the party's popular approach may be seen in the platform which was adopted by the National Aprista Congress of 1931; this program contained a great number of agrarian reform measures, some of a decidedly radical character. The principal items advocated in the party's stated agrarian policy were:

1. A market-reporting service to be created by the state.
2. Legal and economic aid to agriculturists.
3. Compensated expropriation of specified types of farm lands for redistribution, to be used in the production of goods for the internal market.
4. Government regulation of farm tenant contracts.
5. State support and encouragement of collective farms and agricultural cooperatives.
6. Requirements that large farms maintain an accounting system subject to government inspection.
7. Taxation of cultivable but untilled lands.
8. Revision of the systems of irrigation and water rights.
9. Creation of a Ministry of Agriculture.
10. Establishment of agricultural experimental and extension services.
11. Organization of a system of farm and crop insurance.[9]

As can be judged from these measures, the program of the party predicated a strong centralized government, bureaucratically structured. In this regard the policy remained fairly constant during the succeeding years. But there was somewhat greater alteration in other aspects of party doctrine. For one thing, the official attitude toward Yankee imperialism became noticeably less hostile; for another, the party philosophy drifted away not only from the narrower dogmas of the Communist Party but also from the Marxist social and economic interpretations of history.[10]

The membership of APRA continued to grow throughout the 1930's, but the party was never able to gain political dominance. In 1936 the Aprista presidential candidate Luis Eguiguren won the popular majority vote, but the opposition-controlled Constituent Congress annulled the election on the grounds that APRA was an international party and therefore illegal. Combated by both the Benavides dictatorship (1936-1939) and the Prado administration, APRA had little positive voice in the formulation of national policies until the election of the liberal J. L. Bustamante to the presidency in 1946. At this time members of APRA were elected in significant numbers to the Congress, and several were appointed to cabinet posts. Thus entrenched, they were able to initiate legislation which the party had formulated fifteen years previously.

But the newly acquired power was not to last long. In 1948 a political crisis was precipitated by the assassination of a conservative newspaper editor, presumably by Apristas. In the turmoil which ensued the party members holding cabinet positions either resigned or were dismissed. Finally a schism apparently developed within the party itself, so that when the more militant faction attempted a political coup in October, 1948, the uprising failed to receive popular support. The disturbance was quelled, but offered sufficient opportunity for a conservative military group to oust the Bustamante regime on the colorable grounds of "restoring order." The nation found itself again directed by a military *caudillo,* and APRA found itself once more outlawed.

One of the most significant features to be noted in reviewing sociopolitical movements and their influence on agrarian reform is that for the most part such movements have remained in the hands of intellectuals. It might be remembered, however, that the Mexican agrarian revolution also originated with intellectuals and spread only later to the oppressed masses themselves. In Peru APRA has been the only reform party to receive widespread popular support, but it has never been sufficiently strong to override the conservative counterforces. Socialist, Communist, and national reform parties alike have constantly maintained that they had the support of the masses, but to date there has been little evidence to support such assertions.

In the 1920's and early 1930's the functionings of APRA and the Socialist Party were evident in numerous attempts to organize farm laborers. During this period there were many strikes and uprisings of the rural workers on the coast, but little apparent penetration of the movement to the sierra. In some few cases the tenants and laborers won their objectives, but conservative governments generally viewed unions of agricultural workers with disfavor and declared them illegal. Even as early as 1933 a Socialist-backed law regulating owner-tenant relationships was passed by the Congress, but, like other similar liberal legislation, was never actually promulgated. The fates of the Rental Law of 1946 and the *Law of Yanaconaje,* both of which were part of the legislative program of the Apristas during the Bustamante administration, have already been discussed.

The left-wing parties of Peru, like those of the United States, have seen many of their policies adopted by the more conservative groups acquiescing to the evident popularity of various reform measures. About half of the agrarian platform of the 1931 National Aprista Congress, for instance, has since been approved by various national legislatures, none of which could be considered controlled by the Apristas themselves.[11] The apex of contemporary agrarian reform legislation appears to have been reached during the Bustamante administration. Since the accession of the conservative Odría government there has been little open movement of leftist groups and a virtual abandonment of liberal measures previously adopted.

General Remedial Measures

A major reason why radical reform movements have never achieved predicted proportions in Peru is that few national administrations have been totally unresponsive to the plaints of oppressed groups. Nearly every government has accorded some recognition to agrarian problems, and has pledged alleviation. Almost as frequently the promises have remained unfulfilled. Even the reform measures actually promulgated have often been merely paper laws issued more for the pacification of an aroused group than with the sincere intention of application. But honest intent, where it existed, has not been sufficient in itself to lend effectiveness to agrarian legislation in Peru. The frequent changes of administration, each usually accompanied by a wholesale political spoils system, have generally blocked the successful execution of any long-range policy. One who traces the pattern of agrarian legislation can hardly disagree with the bitter statement of the Peruvian economist César Antonio Ugarte that "almost never has a government followed the policies and seconded the plans of its predecessor. Each one has tried to commence anew and, within its ephemeral period, to accomplish projects that required long preparation and more time for execution. . . .

Our agricultural policy can be summed up in a catalog of unfulfilled laws."[12]

Despite the lack of a coordinated and sustained policy, certain broad trends may be recognized as generally or frequently accepted methods by which various administrations have sought to solve the agrarian problems of the nation. These may be grouped under three general classifications: (1) methods of altering the man-land ratio; (2) methods of encouraging and facilitating agricultural production; and (3) methods of increasing productive efficiency. It is not intended that the groupings should be mutually exclusive, since a single measure may clearly serve more than one end. On the whole, though, they are sufficiently inclusive that all the major attempts to deal with agrarian problems in Peru may be cataloged on the basis of their line of approach under one of the three headings, each of which will be analyzed in some greater detail.

Methods of altering the man-land ratio.—The attempts to alter the man-land ratio in Peru may also be grouped under three headings: (1) through redistribution of currently available land among the farming population; (2) through the reduction of the number of persons directly dependent upon the land; (3) through increasing the cultivable area. Examining these in order, we find that the call for redistribution of agricultural lands has probably held the greatest popular appeal in Peru and has been loudly voiced by political parties of all leanings. In fact, its popularity is such that it is embodied in the Peruvian Constitution, Article 47 of which reads:

The state shall favor the preservation and growth of moderate and small rural ownership; it may, by means of a law, and prior indemnification, expropriate lands of private ownership, especially those not being exploited, in order to subdivide them or transfer them under conditions that may be regulated by law.[13]

In addition, Article 211 of the constitution justifies the expropriation of private lands for apportionment to the Indian communities that lack them. Little actual application of either of these measures has been made. Some few haciendas were expropriated in the late 1920's by Leguía, but opponents of the administration maintain that the real beneficiaries of the action were not the Indians but the *hacendados,* who received high recompense for run-down farms. The Prado government also purchased some few farms for redistribution but so sporadically as to suggest a demagogic gesture rather than an instrument of policy.

The widespread belief in land redistribution as a panacea for the nation's agricultural ills has prompted even some liberals to caution against the placing of undue faith in its effectiveness. One such warning was that of Moisés Poblete Troncoso, the Chilean social scientist who investigated social conditions in Peru for the International Labor Office. In his official report he stated:

Many individuals, and especially many Indians, think that the individual apportionment of lands can resolve the agrarian problem. But it is necessary to take into account the technical factor: the isolated Indian, with his primitive tools, has very limited possibilities of cultivating the land profitably. To this must be added his ignorance in the selection of seeds, in the use of fertilizer (which for that matter he cannot buy), etc. The division of the land by itself alone, if it is accomplished, will not be sufficient, because there will be lacking capital, machinery, fertilizer, and a rational organization of production, transport, and marketing.[14]

Such a view, which seems realistic enough, does not deny that land reform is necessary but points out that it is not sufficient in itself to produce the desired social and economic effects.

The second approach to altering the man-land ratio—that of reducing the number of persons directly dependent upon agriculture—has not, strictly speaking, found formulation in any national policy. To date, most persons who have left the land have done so in response to overwhelming economic pressures. But even those who migrate frequently do not yield their possession rights to the land; and they return to it in the planting and harvesting seasons. The rapid growth of urban centers attests, though, that permanent migration is taking place. In every large city of Peru one can find slum areas filled in large part with those who have moved in from rural regions. Some of these are absorbed in industry or construction work, providing a cheap source of manpower. Others subsist only through public relief or private charity. There is reason to believe that the maintenance of a relatively large body of armed forces in the nation is partly to provide employment for a potentially dangerous segment of the rural element while furnishing at the same time an instrument for controlling the remainder. Public works also serve to relieve pressure on the agricultural lands, especially those projects directed toward bringing more land under cultivation. A major government-sponsored program for relieving population pressure on agricultural lands has been the establishment of vocational schools specializing in industrial arts. The effectiveness of this program, which is a relatively recent development, remains to be measured in the future, since it is clearly of a long-range nature.

Two different approaches have been used in the attempt to bring more lands under cultivation in Peru. One has been the engineering of irrigation and drainage projects; the other has been the colonization of undeveloped regions. Thus far the former has been by far the more successful.

The first large irrigation project sponsored by the government was that of the Pampas del Imperial in the Cañete valley, completed in 1923. During the following quarter of a century some 80,000 hectares were added to the agricultural lands of the nation through government irrigation projects in various coastal valleys. Privately sponsored irrigation made usable another 170,000 hectares.[15] The potential acreage that may be made arable through irrigation is tremendous. According to expert estimates, enough water could be stored through the construction of dams and reservoirs to irrigate nearly six million more acres of coastal land.[16] Yet the costs of such projects would be tremendous—so great, according to some authorities, as to be hardly justifiable when measured against the productive worth of the lands thus claimed.[17] Private capitalists are clearly reluctant to underwrite such long-term investments, but the financial considerations involved have seldom curbed the proclamations by national politicos of grandiose schemes to make the desert bloom through irrigation. To cite a typical example, the irrigation program of the Odría administration for improving over one-and-a-half million acres would have cost an estimated 781,500,000 soles, according to the government's own figures, a sum which represented nearly twice the total annual revenue of the national government at the time the program was advocated.

In recent years attention has shifted to the irrigation of sierra valleys, which are normally cultivated with only the water supplied by seasonal rains. These projects do not increase the area of cultivated lands so much as they increase production otherwise restricted by the seasonal nature of the water supply. The relatively lower cost of repressing sierra streams suggests a greater feasibility in this method than in coastal irrigation. The most ambitious engineering of this type to date has been carried out in the Mantaro valley of central Peru.

Strange though it may seem, there are some sections of the coast that actually suffer from an overabundance of water during the rainy season of the sierra. Some of these have been made arable through drainage projects and the construction of reservoirs for controlling the water flow. Drainage projects would also be prerequisite to the successful conversion of much of the selva into agricultural lands. But until improved transportation can make such selvatic agriculture profitable, it is improbable that major operations of this nature will be undertaken.

The inaccessibility of the selva has undoubtedly been a major reason why practically all attempts at colonizing the region have been attended by failure. Beginning in 1849 with utter fiasco of a colony of Germans sent to the department of Loreto, the latter half of the nineteenth century was spattered with a number of disastrous colonization ventures.[18] In 1851 a colony of Irish immigrants failed, but another colony of Germans established at Pozuzo in the department of Huánuco in 1857 was somewhat more fortunate. Lacking communication and transportation facilities to the "outer world," however, the colony was never able to advance beyond a bare subsistence level. A branch of the original Pozuzo group was settled at Oxapampa in 1873, but fared little better. The attempt of some Italian colonists to establish themselves in the selva in 1867 was likewise attended by a marked lack of success. Even the relatively large-scale attempts of the railroad-operating Peruvian Corporation to colonize the Perené valley in the period from 1892 through 1897 had no lasting results.

The philosophy of introducing foreign colonists was founded on the vain hope that trained agriculturists could automatically convert the selva into an economic asset. But most of the foreign colonists, who were brought over by private colonizing companies operating under Peruvian charters, were completely unprepared for the conditions which they were to meet. No few turned back at their first encounter with the jungle. It is to be wondered that some of these isolated groups, completely cut off from the outside world, persisted as long as they did. Yet the recurrent failures did not dim the hopes of some Peruvians that somehow colonists held the magic key to the development of the agricultural potentialities of the region. It is difficult to see what blind faith led them to believe that advanced agricultural techniques would automatically link selva farms with coastal markets, the high sierras notwithstanding.

In the twentieth century, with foreign emigration restricted, attention turned to the possibilities of internal colonization. Significantly enough, such colonization had not developed spontaneously, despite the overcrowded conditions of the sierra farmlands. One reason was that the *hacendados* of the sierra were not anxious to see their labor supply depleted and did not give strong support to such projects. Another was that the selva did not offer the inducements of high wages or city life that the coast could, so most migrants headed westward when they decided to leave home. Only in recent years has the flow to the eastern montaña increased beyond a trickle.

The main impetus to internal colonization was given by the construction of the Lima-Pucallpa highway, begun in the late 1930's and completed in 1945, linking the selva to the coast for the first time with a reasonably passable road for transportation. The most successful colonization attempt thus far in the region served by the highway has been the widely publicized Tingo María venture, established in 1938. Although its early development was retarded by a variety of obstacles, the colony was given a new lease on life through the foundation of an agricultural experiment station under the joint sponsorship of Peru and the United States. By 1950 the population of Tingo María had grown to approximately six thousand. The farmers of the colony are of three types, classified by size of holdings: small farmers with less than 30 hectares; medium farmers with 30 to 100 hectares; and large farmers holding over 100 hectares. These agriculturists are still handicapped by a general lack of labor and modern farm equipment. The larger farmers have been particularly affected by these shortages, in some cases to the extent that the requirement that a minimum of 10 per cent of the grant be under cultivation has been violated.[19] Thus, even in this most promising case, it appears too early to pronounce the program of internal colonization an unqualified success. The experimental station and associated farm extension service centered at Tingo María are certainly necessary preliminaries to the successful colonization of the selva, though, as much as the highway itself. The success attained by more recent attempts at foreign colonization initiated with the establishment of an Italian group at Oxapampa should prove a good test of whether conditions are now ripe for the realization of an old Peruvian dream.

Methods of encouraging and facilitating agricultural production.—A second category of general remedial measures to be considered is that concerned with increasing agricultural production. Certainly one of the most serious economic problems which Peru has faced in recent times has been the failure of its agriculture to keep abreast of consumption and demand. The critical nature of this problem has forced the adoption of a variety of measures aimed at removing some of the major handicaps faced by the agricultural and ranching industries.

A basic difficulty which has plagued Peruvian agriculture—and a general affliction of farmers in nearly every nation, for that matter—has been the lack of operating capital. Agricultural enterprises normally require a relatively high outlay of money at the beginning of the planting season, and this is frequently obtained through loans. Without venturing into the theory of credit risks, suffice it to say that farm and ranching enterprises are subject to a number of uncontrollable factors that increase the interest rates on such capital as credit firms are willing to advance. When property and equipment are used as collateral security for such loans, which is frequently the case, the farmer stands the chance of losing his only means of redemption as the result of a single bad year.

Before 1931, Peruvian farmers could obtain credit only from private sources, some of which charged completely usurious interest rates. In many cases no credit at all could be obtained. The consequence of capital shortages in terms of special tenancy arrangements has already been discussed. Frequently the landless were forced to seek advances from the proprietor of the land they worked, or loans which were to be paid after the harvest with 50 to 100 per cent interest.

In 1931, the Banco Agrícola del Perú was established for the purpose of making low-interest loans available to agriculturists. The working resources of the bank were provided through a 10 million *sol* appropriation by the national government. The bank was not actually able to begin operations until 1933, in which year it made only seven loans. Fifteen years later, though, its annual volume of business was measured at nearly 6,000 loans involving more than 62 million *soles*. The rapid expansion of the bank's activities has been attended by some formidable problems, most of which are traceable to insufficient operating capital. The policy of the bank has been to make controlled credit loans, usually with crop security. Loans of this type are for stipulated purposes which the bank directors consider safe investments, and the close control has undoubtedly been responsible for the relatively small losses suffered through bad loans. During its first seventeen years of operation losses amounted to less than 1 per cent of the total loans made.[20] At the same time, however, the application of a controlled credit policy increases the operating expenses of the bank, particularly where direct small loans are involved which require higher control costs in proportion to the amount loaned. This is the type of loan which most small farmers seek, and it was for them primarily that the bank was established, inasmuch as they are less likely to obtain loans from private banks. By restricting its operations the bank might have been able to meet even these relatively high costs under established interest rates. But in order to broaden its services the bank loaned more money than was provided by government appropriations, by means of borrowing from other banks. Even though it borrowed at an interest rate of 3 per cent, the bank could charge only 5 per cent (increased to 6 per cent in 1948), and the difference failed to cover the costs of operation. As a result, the bank steadily lost money despite a phenomenally low incidence of bad loans. Finally, in 1950, when it appeared that the bank would be forced to curtail the number of its loans, a government decree was issued raising the authorized capital of the bank from 25 million to 100 million *soles*. The effectiveness of this measure depends upon how much of the authorized capital is actually placed at the disposal of the bank. One of the difficulties of past years has been that available funds have seldom exceeded 50 per cent of those legally authorized.

In the 1948-1949 fiscal year, loans to small farmers accounted for approximately 37 per cent of the total amount loaned and about 90 per cent of the total number of loans, the highest proportions to that time.[21] Yet even these so-called small farmers do not represent the most needy elements of the farm population. The Indians, for instance, are as yet receiving practically no financial aid from this source. Furthermore, it seems certain that, until the bank is able to achieve sufficient stability to extend its services to them, the class of farmers most desperately in need is not likely to find any new solution to their pressing credit problems.

Another advocated solution for the production problems of the nation's small farmers has been the organization of agricultural cooperatives of various types. But so far there has been little action taken in this direction and less success achieved. The cooperative movement in Peru dates from 1902, when the National Congress authorized the promulgation of an "organic cooperative law."[22] Under the Constitution of 1933 the government assumed the obligation of furthering the cooperative movement, and in 1941 a section of agricultural cooperatives was created in the Ministry of Agriculture.

The mortality rate of the few cooperatives which have actually been established in Peru has been high. In 1950 only thirty-four were listed on the rolls of the Ministry of Agriculture. Of these, seventeen were producer cooperatives, twelve consumer, one credit, and four of a general service nature. The establishment of credit cooperatives has long been encouraged by the Banco Agrícola, but the statistics clearly reveal that the suggestion has not been widely heeded.

The idea of organizing the Indian communities on a modern cooperative basis has frequently been advanced in Peru, but seldom effected.

Some few instances do exist, such as the communities of Chupaca, described by Sáenz, and Muquiyauyo, investigated by Castro Pozo and by Tschopik.[23] Within these communities are organizations called "institutions," which operate on a cooperative basis. According to Tschopik's description

. . . each Institution [sociopolitical unit] owns tracts which were formerly *cofradías* of the community. The fields of each Institution are planted, cultivated, and harvested communally by the members of the Institution, and either the produce is divided or the crops are sold and the profits shared among those who have contributed with their own labor. In addition, the Institutions own communal grazing lands in the mountainous annex of Los Andes and elsewhere within the district, and taxes are collected from members who herd their livestock in these pastures. . . .[24]

The spread of the cooperative movement in the sierra is also to be seen in the establishment of communal herds of purebred sheep under the auspices of the Junta Nacional de las Industrias Lanares. The herds belonging to Indian communities are numerous but generally of poor quality, and it has been the aim of this national organization to improve wool production through the replacement of degenerate stock with the purebred. Reported results from this project have thus far been highly favorable, but these can be considered only progress reports because of the long-term nature of the undertaking.

It should be made clear that these reported examples of cooperatives established within the Indian communities depict exceptional instances rather than the general case. The fact that the communities have maintained a tradition of cooperative action in many of their economic tasks does not necessarily qualify them to organize and operate successful cooperatives. Modern cooperatives are essentially business enterprises requiring able administration by the leaders and full understanding and support by the members. Until Indian farmers are trained in basic methods of business management—a yet distant realization, to judge from their current educational status—the prediction of any considerable success for such organizations would appear an act of boundless optimism.

Another major barrier to increased agricultural productivity in Peru has been, and is, the gross inadequacy of the nation's transportation facilities. Clearly there can be no incentive to market production if it is impossible to move perishable agricultural goods to a market. Yet as late as the third decade of the twentieth century the chief mode of transport in the sierra was the llama pack train, the same system employed by the Incas. Coastal transportation at that time was primarily by sea routes, since few of the valleys were connected by either railroads or highways.

Railroad construction was begun as early as 1851 in Peru, when the effects of the guano boom were first beginning to be felt. Some of the most awe-inspiring engineering feats of modern times were performed by the ingenious Yankee Henry Meiggs in the building of railroads from the coast to 15,000-foot sierra heights.[25] Despite the financial collapse of Peru as a result of the war with Chile, some 1,800 kilometers of lines were completed by the turn of the century. During the first half of the twentieth century more than 2,200 kilometers of track, including spur lines, were laid. Three principal lines connect the coast with the sierra. One of these is in the south and two are in the central section, while the extreme north has no major railroad system. High construction costs and relatively low returns, especially since the competition of motor trucks has increased, serve to retard the laying of other lines. Construction was begun in 1950 on a new line to the town of Pucallpa in the upper selva. If completed, it will serve the new region of colonization in the Huallaga valley. Otherwise, prospects of further expansion of rail transportation are not great.

Modern highway construction in Peru did not really get under way until the second administration of Leguía, from 1919 to 1930. Some road building had been done prior to that time, of course, but under Leguía the Roadway Conscription Act was passed, which required male citizens to work a specified number of days on road construction projects in their provinces or pay for the hiring of a substitute. This act was later repealed when it became simply another instrument of exploitation, but it did mark the increased interest in establishing transportation links.

As late as 1936 there were only 242 kilometers of hard-surfaced roads in the entire country, with 1,200 kilometers of improved roadbeds of other types. Another 1,500 kilometers of hard-surfaced road were added with the completion of the Peruvian section of the Pan-American Highway connecting Ecuador with Chile by way of the coast. By 1946 the country had approximately 2,700 kilometers of paved or asphalted roads, 23,500 kilometers of other types of improved roads, and 8,000 kilometers of unimproved surfaces.[26] A project to complete a longitudinal highway in the sierra, following closely the famous highland route of the Inca Empire, has never been completed. The existing sections of this road, however, have been connected with the Pan-American Highway by a dozen transverse links.

Of three proposed east-west transcontinental highways, only one had been completed by 1950. That was the central route connecting the coastal port of Callao with the Amazon port of Pucallpa on the Ucayali River. The upkeep of this road, which passes through Tingo María and is intended to serve the new colonization region, has proved extremely difficult and expensive. As a consequence, traffic flow has been far below expectations, which probably encouraged the laying of the new railway to Pucallpa. The projected northern transcontinental highway joining the coastal city of Chiclayo with the port of Prado on the navigable Marañon was about half completed in 1950. The southern route has been completed from the Pacific port of Matarani through Arequipa and Cuzco to the town of Inambari in the high selva. Further construction is expected to extend the route to Puerto Maldonado on the Madre de Dios River.[27]

The topographical features of Peru make road construction and maintenance exceedingly expensive. There is a constant battle on the coast to keep the desert sands from completely burying the roadways. In the sierra the steep and broken terrain requires the most resourceful engineering for initial construction, while landslides frequently block the ways for periods of weeks. The selva, too, is hostile to road building, with seasonal floods washing out roadbeds and lush vegetation seeking to blot out all such evidences of industrial civilization. Only air transportation seems able to surmount most of these handicaps imposed by nature, but the cost of air freight precludes its extensive use in agriculture at the present.

In spite of their limited development the modern transportation facilities of Peru should not be underestimated in their influence upon social and cultural change. It would be no exaggeration to say that the provision of road and rail transport has contributed more to the acculturation of the sierra Indians than all the educational programs of church and government to date. The motor truck, especially, has provided a means for the Indian to transport his wares to market swiftly and cheaply enough to realize a profit on his dealings. It has brought many previously isolated regions into relatively close contact with a larger world for the first time in the history of the nation, and has opened new horizons of attainment to their inhabitants. No one who has seen the women of Indian communities proudly wearing skirts of purchased velvet, the men who have donned Western dress, the children playing with manufactured toys purchased on a trip to the city, can deny the influence of powerful cultural factors. It seems clear that new desires have been and are being awakened through the wider range of contacts now made possible, and that the development of a new value system is prerequisite to the stimulation of greater economic productivity on the part of the Indian element.

Methods of increasing productive efficiency.—The agricultural production problems of Peru stem from more than the shortage and inequitable distribution of land, important as these factors are. They are also resultants of economic policies, land utilization, and farming techniques; and solutions to these problems predicate not only the supplying of materials necessary to efficient agriculture but also technical training of the farm population. Neither materials nor training have yet been supplied in any appreciable quantity, but the nation is become increasingly aware of their necessity.

Vocational agricultural education is scarcely more prevalent than any other types of formal education in rural Peru. The census findings of 1940 revealed, as previously pointed out, the virtual absence of schooling in many rural sierra provinces. Prior to the tabulation of these census data—although no doubt stimulated by foreknowledge of what would be shown—the national legislature passed in 1941 a public education law which included among its other provisions stipulations for the establishment of training schools in rural regions.[28] The need for providing this type of training had been publicly recognized as early as 1920, when agricultural schools had been provided in various provinces. These, however, were geographically dispersed and served only a small portion of the entire farming population. Even in 1946 the total matriculation in nineteen *colegios agropecuarios* was less than 600 students, while three agricultural technical schools had an enrollment of slightly more than 100. The Escuela Nacional de Agricultura, equivalent to an agricultural college, had at the time some 400 students enrolled, but 70 per cent of those were from the two departments of Lima and Arequipa.[29] Hence, its value to the entire nation was somewhat limited.

The most recent attempts to meet rural educational needs have involved international cooperative efforts. One of these was the formulation of a joint educational campaign to be carried out by Peru and Bolivia in the Lake Titicaca basin. As part of this program a number of "scholastic centers" were established in the Lake Titicaca and Urubamba River regions, beginning in 1946. By 1950 there were sixteen main schools with 364 branch units operating in various communities. The curriculum provided for both adults and children was centered around the teaching of Spanish, basic principles of hygiene, agriculture, stock raising, and domestic arts. The reported total enrollment in these schools after only four years of operation was 3,600.[30]

Another international program was developed through an agreement with the United States in 1946 which established the Servicio Cooperativo Peruano-Norteamericano de Educación. Under the terms of the agreement the Inter-American Educational Foundation of the Institute of Inter-American Affairs provided specialists and equipment for a technical training program, especially in undeveloped areas.[31] The most extensive work of the agency by 1950 had been in the Mantaro valley of the central sierra. There prevocational training was begun in thirty-two rural schools in anticipation of establishing more advanced courses at a later date. A new agreement was signed in 1949, which provided for extending the prevocational program to other rural regions throughout the nation.

Another line of attack on the agricultural production problems of Peru has been the relatively recent development of agricultural experiment stations and extension services. The first organized experimental work was initiated with the establishment of the Escuela Nacional de Agricultura in 1902, and the operation of sugar cane and cotton experimental stations began in 1906[32] The first major experimental farm was founded in 1928 at La Molina by the Sociedad Nacional Agraria and was later taken over by the national government. A Ministry of Agriculture was established in the government in 1943; this new administrative branch undertook the supervision of about a dozen experiment stations, most of which also offered limited extension service. In recent years the efficiency of the government agricultural service program has been considerably reduced by the frequent changes of technical personnel with the ebb and flow of political tides. In more than a few instances "political losses" reduced the already scarce number of trained technicians to the point where experimental operations virtually ceased.

As in the case of its educational problems, Peru has sought aid for its agricultural experimental and extension services through international agreements. The most important agreement of this nature led to the establishment in 1943 of the Servicio Cooperativo Inter-Americano de Producción de Alimentos, of which frequent mention has been made in preceding pages. SCIPA, as the organization is generally known in Peru, is another project of the Institute of Inter-American Affairs. It has, since founding, operated as an autonomous unit within the Ministry of Agriculture under the direction of a North American administrator, who also serves as head of the Food Production Mission of the I.I.A.A.

The primary stimulus to the establishment of SCIPA was the critical food shortage which developed in Peru during World War II as a result of the curtailment of food imports. At that time a broad program was instituted which consisted not only of projects aimed at alleviating the immediate situation but also of long-range designs to cope with various basic problems. After the termination of the war the program was continued along lines recommended by technical experts of the organization who had made surveys of the national agrarian situation from various angles. The main projects of SCIPA which either had been completed or were in process in 1950 may be sumarized as follows:

1. Numerous economic studies of fundamental agrarian problems, as the bases for programs of remedial action.

2. Various engineering and land-use developments, consisting of building construction where necessary, and the sponsorship of irrigation, drainage, land rehabilitation, and soil conservation projects.

3. Provision of facilities and services for agriculturists, including farm tools and machines, fertilizers and insecticides, imported breeding stock, farm equipment pools, distribution of essential crop and vegetable seeds, allocation of funds for other essential equipment, and the guidance and supervision of new technical operations.

4. Organization of a national agricultural extension service, which consisted in 1950 of thirty-one rural agencies in various regions of the country, serving to disseminate technical information and services and to provide home demonstrations in nutrition and home management.

5. Establishing in many rural sections of *Clubs Agrícolas Juveniles* similar in nature and purpose to the 4-H Clubs of the United States.

6. Operation of a nutrition and dietetics service. This service investigates national dietary habits and suggests measures for improvement. A demonstration program of diet and nutrition education has been provided for homes and schools.

7. Home and school garden programs for increasing national vegetable production.

8. Improvement of food storage resources through the construction of new warehouses, the repair of deteriorated storage buildings, and the provision of technical advice to private individuals constructing their own storage facilities.[33]

The accomplishments of SCIPA, in the judgment of the writer, have been notable. Trips made with extension agents in various regions of the country revealed some impressive transformations in regard to both land use and cultivation techniques. The fact that the program is on a voluntary basis, though, has meant that most of the aid has been given to farmers who were already relatively well trained. Very little has been done for the Indian group, whose needs in this respect are by far the greatest in the country. On one occasion the author questioned members of an Indian community living within twenty-five miles of a SCIPA extension agency as to whether they had ever made use of its facilities. They had never heard of it. The local head of the agency was then queried as to whether aid was extended to Indians in the area. He replied that aid was given to all who requested it, but added, significantly, that few Indians had ever made requests.

Despite its limitations, the SCIPA program does appear to offer real promise to Peruvian agriculture. But since it has never operated under contracts of more than three years' duration, the organization could hardly be considered a permanent feature. Furthermore, much of its success seems to stem from its efficient organization, able administration, and adequate supply of operating funds. It is highly questionable whether all or any of these characteristics can be retained when and if the organization passes completely under Peruvian control, an ultimate objective of the Institute of Inter-American Affairs. The fact that many of SCIPA's attainments have been possible only because of its freedom from the traditional political interference in government bureau staffing and operations would seem to justify considerable doubts as to its future if this independence is lost.

The cooperation of Peru and the United States in the maintenance of an agricultural station at Tingo María has already been mentioned.[34] This was effected through an agreement made between the United States Department of Agriculture and the Peruvian Ministry of Agriculture, with both nations supplying technicians and materials.[35] The main functions of the station have been concerned with developing products and techniques suitable to agriculture in the selva. The extension service provided has been mainly for the colony of Tingo María itself, since there are not many other settlements operating under similar environmental conditions. The experimental research being conducted now should prove of inestimable benefit if colonization expectations are ever fully realized. In fact, it may determine whether extensive colonization of the selva will be feasible at all. The very future of the entire region and with it the economic hopes of a nation may well hinge on this one experimental station.

An adequate appraisal of the effectiveness of agrarian reform actions in Peru presents a difficult task at the present time. There are, to be sure, no currently visible signs of any strong sociopolitical movements dedicated toward this end, but this does not necessarily mean that they can be completely discounted. It is not easy to stamp out the flaming ideas of such men as González Prada, Mariátegui, and Haya de la Torre, however firmly the organizations which they inspired might be suppressed. Nor can it be maintained that their preachments were completely unavailing; many of the reforms for which they called, and which in their time were considered extreme, have since been quietly incorporated into national policy. But, in truth, their more direct accomplishments were few, largely because the brightly burning intellectual fuses did not reach the potentially explosive proletarian masses. Only the Alianza Popular Revolucionaria Americana received widespread popular support, but even that group could not attain a position of national political dominance.

Slightly greater success may be claimed for a variety of remedial measures directed toward the solution of specific agrarian problems. Yet their effectiveness has been considerably restricted because they have typically been independent acts rather than parts of an integrated program. Greater coordination has been achieved by such organizations as SCIPA through the development of long-range policies and objectives. But their operations have begun so recently that all except the most tentative evaluations would be premature. There have been too many programs abruptly curtailed in the past by changes in political administration to make predictions of success appear other than venturesome.

The lack of an effectual land policy cannot be overestimated in its consequences. It is difficult to see how new agricultural techniques can make much headway in solving production problems so long as the fundamental problems of land distribution remain unsolved. And the same is true of other peripheral approaches; they seem foredoomed to failure unless they are able to set in motion forces that will produce the necessary alterations in the land pattern. The reluctance to make a frontal attack on the land issue is not merely a matter of deference to large landowners and the latifundian tradition, as many have supposed. It must be realized that these are not problems for which pat solutions can be offered. Peruvian politicians are prone to leave such questions to be answered by the course of circumstance—an inaction which finds ready rationalization in terms of "natural economic laws." But if they are willing to let circumstance answer the question, they must realize that similar circumstances have provided grim responses. Hard-pressed and frustrated men have risen in bloody rebellion because they felt they had no more to lose, and they have rebelled not against formless circumstance but against those who allowed impersonal forces to hold sway.

The optimistic assumption that the process of industrialization will somehow effect satisfactory solutions to the problems of rural Peru may not be completely unfounded. Certainly foreign capitalists and technicians have provided considerable assistance toward the development of various regions. Nevertheless, to consign the economic future of the nation to their tender mercies appears an act of blind and boundless trust. The adoption of a laissez-faire attitude with respect to the agrarian economy may not prove positively deleterious, but there seems little reason to expect as a consequence social returns that are exclusively, or even predominantly, beneficial.

7.

The Changing Scene

INDUSTRIALIZATION is effecting in Peru, as it has throughout a major portion of the Western world, a radical transformation and integration of society and culture. The ultimate outcome one can at best only conjecture. Conjectures need not be wild guesses, however. There is good reason to expect that many of the changes which industrialization has brought about in other nations will occur also in Peru. It is also reasonable to expect certain unique modifications as a result of the individual characteristics of Peruvian society and culture. With these factors considered, the probabilities of making good guesses are improved, even though the technique is not sufficiently refined to deserve the label of "scientific prediction." A further aid, and perhaps the most valuable, to successful speculation is the detection of trends which seem already established and which may be extrapolated to some plausible conclusions. It is obviously impossible to consider all the details of the complex situation which is evolving, but the apparent direction of some of the broader and deeper movements may be roughly sketched. The special orientation of this study suggests as logical base points for a summary analysis of the changing Peruvian scene the population and the man-land relational system.

The Peruvian population appears to be responding in a classic manner to the introduction of the scientific accompaniments of industrialization in the forms of sanitation and medical techniques. Despite the restricted spread of these practices, particularly in the highlands, where they have yet to reach some of the more inaccessible regions, they have been largely responsible for the doubling of the national

144

population during the first half of the twentieth century. Should the current estimated growth rate of 2 per cent per year continue, the population will again double in thirty-five years. Actually, there is every reason to expect the growth rate to increase as sanitary engineering, medical knowledge, and public health measures become more extensively adopted. Barring famine, epidemics, and similar disasters, the population may reach the 16 million mark long before 1985.

The effects of the increasing population load on the limited supply of arable land are to be seen in the development of a variety of conditions, some of which present critical problems. By 1950 there was already less than half an acre of cultivated land per inhabitant, and the prospects for bringing any vast new areas under cultivation in the near future are not great. Fractionalization of holdings has occurred in many places to the extent that the land quotients are far too small to yield a subsistence to their owners. The process has been furthered, although by no means caused, by the relatively recent growth of large-scale commercial farms. In reality, most of these have grown through the incorporation of already large haciendas, so it is doubtful that they have radically altered the previously existing pattern of distribution, at least so far as the land in small farms is concerned. There is, nevertheless, a widespread belief in many rural sections that the process of subdivision being felt with increasing severity is attributable to the expansion of corporate farms rather than to the increase in rural population. Valid or not, this belief may some day serve as the rationale for a program of expropriation and redistribution of large holdings, the traditional remedy offered for this particular ill. As even many of the leaders of land reform movements in Peru have realized, the breaking up of productive commercial estates would deal a severe blow to the economy, and, for that matter, would provide only temporary relief if the rural population continued to swell.

There can be little doubt, though, that the mincing of the farm land to the extent that it has taken place in much of Peru—for whatever reasons—has led to productive inefficiency. Considerable acreage is wasted just through utilizing uncultivated land strips as plot boundaries. The greatest obstacles to efficiency are not physical, great as these are, but social. The sheer number of owners in some cases is enough to increase the probabilities of social discord. Even more upsetting, however, is the fact that they are operating under conditions of strain which would make harmonious relations difficult under optimum physical conditions. On the surface it may appear that the tremendous investments of time and money in land litigations reflect only the confusion of many owners and more boundaries. More deeply, though, they reveal the true extent of insecurity and frustration translated into aggression and adding to the general disorganization. When cooperation is most needed, it is least to be had.

The downward spiral of productivity is difficult to treat with technological knowledge alone, as the representatives of the cooperative food mission in Peru have learned. Between 1939 and 1949 the value of national food imports increased 75 per cent, substantially more than the value of all nonfood imports. The very population growth that calls for a higher food production simultaneously introduces conditions which retard the productive process. The result is that Peru, still considered primarily an agricultural nation, is already heavily dependent upon other countries for its food supply.

A major effect of the rising man-land ratio has been that of a stimulus to migration, especially from rural sections of the sierra. A small proportion of the migrants have gone eastward to the upper selva, hoping thus to cling to their agrarian heritage. Certainly this area holds the greatest hopes for increasing the national farm acreage, but the realization of colonization aspirations still lies, as it has always lain, in the unspecified future. The greatest movement has been to the coastal valleys, where limited opportunities for agricultural laborers are available, and to the cities of both the coast and the sierra. This siphoning off of surplus population has not been sufficient to alleviate the land problem, nor is it likely to be in the near future. The land and community ties of the Indians, especially, are powerful, being severed only under the direst stress. Even those who depart, frequently retain legal title to their meager holdings, so their leaving contributes nothing to the solution of the problems of excessively small divisions.

At the risk of digression, it seems necessary to give some explanation for the rising status of farm tenants under conditions which hardly seem conducive to upward social mobility. It would seem logical that the oversupply of rural population would produce the opposite effect. To some extent the gains registered may be attributed to political pressures, but it must also be recalled that the legislation passed for the benefit of tenants in 1946 and 1947—the high point of the most recent liberal political movement—was never successfully applied. The landowners, although recognizing the necessity for making concessions to the tenant classes, were still sufficiently powerful to control the types of concessions to be made. Their acquiescence was, therefore, not so much to political forces as to economic.

The most plausible explanation for the tenant gains would then appear to lie in the changing nature of the economy. Under the "colonial" economy, which persevered well into the republican era, the major symbol of affluence was land possession. But under a capitalist system mere ownership is not enough; production is an equal, if not more important, criterion of success. As production has gained in honorific value, producers have gained in functional value. Hence the increased demand for productive tenants—and in Peru, despite the abundance of rural workers, really productive tenants are rare. This condition does not reflect any innate ineptitude. It is the normal consequence of several hundred years of indifference or exploitation on the part of landowners who neither expected nor received efficient operation of their farms. Now, when they are sorely needed, trained agriculturists are at a premium and competition for their services is high.

The land and population situation has produced two problem groups in Peru, or, perhaps more accurately, one such group in two different places: a backward agricultural peasantry and an unskilled industrial proletariat. The former have entrusted their future to the hope that their familiar situation will improve; the latter have sought a new situation, but their future, too, is otherwise beyond their control.

The main handicap of the migrant group is their lack of technical training. Even on the corporate farms mechanization has reduced the demand for unskilled labor almost to a minimum. At the same time, the larger estates must still depend largely upon foreign or foreign-trained personnel to fill the roles of business managers, agronomists, and similar positions requiring special skills. The same situation prevails in cities, where a shortage of trained technicians exists and a surfeit of unskilled laborers. Programs of education and vocational training will eventually settle this predicament, but before that time conditions may reach an acute stage.

The development of an industrial proletariat from an agricultural peasantry is a disturbing, and frequently dangerous, process. With a limited demand for their services, the great masses of unskilled migrants are in a poor bargaining position for raising their economic status, even should they obtain jobs. Labor history of western Europe and North America is replete with examples of similar situations, with managerial policy justifying the low wages paid on the grounds of the "natural" law of supply and demand. Undoubtedly such a policy has hastened the organization of labor unions, which many managerial groups, in keeping with their former logic, view as artificial barriers raised against the operation of "natural" economic laws.

It would be a distortion of facts to call the paternalistic treatment accorded Peruvian workers on the commercial farms (and probably in many of the urban industries as well) exploitative. In truth, the wages and laboring conditions provided are considerably better than those to which agricultural workers in the country have been accustomed for centuries past. But, as managerial groups have learned in the more highly industrialized countries, paternalism has its limits. To the Peruvian *colono* from the highlands it may appear a just policy and, certainly, a tremendous improvement over his previous situation. A new generation, however, will judge it not in terms of past conditions, which they will not have experienced, but rather in terms of new aspirations. The hard pressed, landless farmer may accept paternalistic offerings with gratitude, but the worldly-wise industrial laborer rejects them disdainfully or angrily as gilded instruments of exploitation.

It is not difficult to see why managerial groups are anxious to "protect" their workers from the labor organizers whose arguments are intended to produce dissatisfaction with conditions now considered acceptable. The stand of management has, for the most part, been strongly backed by the national government, which has suppressed leaders and movements considered antagonistic to business and industrial dominance, on the ostensible grounds of their being either communist or communist-inspired. This repressive policy has undoubtedly retarded the development of any strong labor movement, but equally significant has been the fact that most labor leaders have been too far removed, physically and intellectually, from those to whom they would appeal. Their arguments have been pitched to a more sophisticated level than that of the contemporary proletariat, and hence have continued to receive their most vociferous approbation from university students. As the laboring classes become more conscious of the outer world and its values, the seeds of discontent may find a more receptive soil.

It is not to be assumed that cultural and social changes are restricted to the cities and coastal rural areas where commercialized agriculture has taken hold. Even in the more remote regions of the highlands the cultural complexion is changing as traditional barriers are being destroyed. Improved transportation and communication are rapidly widening the range of social and cultural contacts for thousands of villages, and are serving to dissipate the ignorance and provincialism that have so long held sway. Moreover, there are few families that do not have some member who has gone to the city, either as an army conscript or because of the land shortage. Many of these have returned to relate their experiences and to spread their information and misinformation about life in other regions. In addition, the formal educational programs, which today are still in the embryonic stage, may be counted on to hasten the transformation process in the future.

The same factors which are reducing the spatial and social isolation of rural communities are also operating to produce a more homogeneous society. A major reason for the failure of land reform and Pan-Indian movements to take hold in the past has been the lack of awareness on the part of individual community groups that their problems were common with those of other locality groups. Modern communication and transportation should make possible this realization, but whether organization and action will follow is a matter of speculation. If a social movement does develop, there is a strong likelihood that it will find root and expression in the system of man-land relations. Not only does the land system offer a clearly perceptible source of misery, but it also symbolizes the traditional subordinate status of the rural masses, in particular the Indians. It might well be that by the time a program of land reform could be implemented, it would be a functional anachronism, a Pyrrhic victory gained for purely symbolic reasons at a dreadful economic cost. The history of humankind is filled with such ironic tragedies.

If there were any organized social revolutionary movements under way in Peru at mid-century, they were well concealed. Quite probably there were none; or if there were, they were of a small-scale nature. Yet the social and economic state of the nation is such that the possibility of some future upheaval cannot be completely discounted. Rural peoples living under far better conditions than those of many Peruvians have risen in angry protest when circumstances made such action appear feasible and just. The adoption of new values can easily brand as intolerable the conditions of life once accepted as the normal lot of a peasantry. Justification for revolutions is frequently made in terms of past injuries, many of which have become injuries only through recent definitions. When this is the case, last-minute concessions of rights and privileges have little arresting effect but serve rather to lend substance to the allegation of previous mistreatment, thus adding fuel to the fire.

The major problem of Peru in this critical era is that of developing an industrial middle class into which the proletarian masses can be absorbed. Unless they can be provided with channels for gaining prestige and economic security in the new society, these lower classes will undoubtedly create some disturbance. There is some misconception that the industrialization process automatically creates a middle class. Actually, the establishment of a wage scale that will make such a development possible has nearly always come in response to either threatened or actual violence on the part of labor. Business and industrial interests, although they have almost invariably profited in the long run from the creation of an internal market which a prosperous middle class provides, have more often than not persisted in viewing wages as a production cost to be kept at a minimum rather than as an investment in market expansion which yields indirect returns proportional to the amounts invested. Prosperous industries are necessary to a prosperous society in an industrial age, but they do not, in themselves, provide any guarantees that the general welfare will be served. Especially is this true in such countries as Peru, where the controlling ownership of stocks and bonds is concentrated in the hands of foreign investors and a narrow stratum of the national society. Under such conditions the apparent belief of some Peruvian leaders that financial manipulations benefiting the business and industrial groups will alone somehow solve all the underlying social and economic problems appears naïve, to say the least.

There is no reason why the rural peoples of Peru cannot be introduced into a twentieth-century industrial system with a minimum of disturbance through a well coordinated program of social and economic action administered under capable leadership. But the failure to comprehend fully the nature and magnitude of the changes which are taking place is perilous. Equally dangerous is a policy which raises the hopes and expectations of the citizenry beyond the possibilities of achievement. The possibilities of a peaceful transition are good, but a national policy that is disjointed, indifferent, or discriminatory can easily provoke a reaction of incalculable violence. Neither course is inevitable; either is possible. Theoretically, the choice may lie with the Peruvian people; actually, it lies with their national leaders.

Notes

1.

1. Perú, Ministerio de Hacienda y Comercio, Dirección nacional de Estadística, *Censo nacional de Población y Ocupación, 1940,* Vol. I: *Resúmenes generales* (Lima, 1944), cxcv, cuadro 3. (Hereinafter cited as *Censo nacional.*)

2. For a full explanation of the coastal meteorological phenomena see Isaiah Bowman, *The Andes of Southern Peru: Geographical Reconnaissance along the Seventy-third Meridian* (New York, 1916), pp. 125-147.

3. Javier Pulgar Vidal, "Las ocho Regiones naturales del Perú," *Boletín del Museo de Historia natural "Javier Prado,"* V, 17 (2nd trimester, 1941), 145-160.

4. Pedro E. Paulet, "Las cinco Regiones del Perú," *Peruanidad,* I, 1 (November, 1941), 5-12; Emilio Romero, *Geografía económica del Perú* (Lima, 1939), p. 504.

5. Technically, the use of the term "knot" is incorrect, as pointed out by Preston E. James in his *Latin America* (Revised edition, New York, 1950). Professor James states: "It is definitely incorrect to describe the Peruvian Andes as composed of three or four parallel cordilleras, like the Andes of Colombia. On many maps the stream divides are shown as mountain ranges, and places where many streams rise are represented as 'knots'. The facts are quite different. Actually, the several ranges are not continuous and are generally arranged in echelon with no connection between the separate rows of peaks. The idea of the mountain knot should be dropped entirely from the description of the Andes" (p. 135). Since Professor James does not offer any more suitable term for the areas now described as knots, the designation has been preserved here as being descriptive, if not technically accurate.

6. *Censo nacional, 1940,* I, clxv. The Peruvian census considered as urban ". . . those residing in the capitals of civil divisions [*departamentos, provincias,* and *distritos*] and those who live in populated centers whose number of inhabitants exceeds the arithmetic average of the population of the capitals, providing they do not have typically rural characteristics [haciendas, *fundos, comunidades,* etc.] . . . ."

7. *Ibid.,* I, cxix. Unfortunately, the age data are particularly unreliable because of ignorance and conscious distortion—a fact which restricts the utility of computations made from them.

8. *Ibid.,* I, cv, cuadro 2. Exact figure: 20.31 per thousand.

153

9. United Nations, *Demographic Yearbook, 1951* (New York, 1952), p. 201, Table 14.

10. *Ibid.*, pp. 330-331, Table 19.

11. *Censo nacional, 1940*, I, 55.

12. *Demographic Yearbook*, 1951, p. 271, Table 16.

13. *Censo nacional, 1940*, I, 138, cuadro 33.

14. *Ibid.*, I, 466, cuadro 146.

15. Bernard Mishkin, "The Contemporary Quechua," *The Andean Civilizations*, Vol. II of *Handbook of South American Indians*, Smithsonian Institution, U. S. Bureau of American Ethnology, Bulletin 143 (Washington, 1946), p. 414.

2.

1. Horatio Urteaga, *El Imperio incaico en el que se incluye la Historia del Ayllu y Familia de los Incas* (Lima, 1931), p. 32.

2. John H. Rowe has characterized the *ayllu* of the Incas as being theoretically endogamous, patrilineal, and without totemism. He further states, "There is no historical or ethnological evidence to support the theory that the social group from which the *ayllu* developed was, in some prehistoric era, a true clan. . . ." ("Inca Culture at the Time of the Spanish Conquest," *Handbook of South American Indians*, II, 255.)

3. Bautista Saavedra,*El Ayllu*, 2nd ed. (Santiago de Chile, 1938), p. 162.

4. Heinrich Cunow, *Las Comunidades de Aldea y de Marca del Perú antiguo*, trans. María Woitscheck (Paris, 1929), p. 40.

5. Cunow, *La Organización social del Imperio de los Incas*, trans. María Woitscheck (Lima, 1933), pp. v-vi.

6. Cf. José Mejía Valera, *Organización de la Sociedad en el Perú precolombino, hasta la Aparición del Estado Inka* (Lima, 1946), pp. 182-183.

7. Philip Ainsworth Means, *Ancient Civilizations of the Andes* (New York, 1942), p. 171.

8. Max Uhle, "Desarrollo y Origen de las Civilizaciones americanas" (reprint from *Proceedings of the Twenty-third International Congress of Americanists* [September, 1928]), pp. 31-43. Cf. also Uhle, *Las antiguas Civilizaciones de Manta* (Quito, 1931), *passim.*

9. Julio C. Tello, *Origen y Desarrollo de las Civilizaciones prehistóricas andinas* (Lima, 1942), *passim.*

10. Means, *passim.*

11. Rowe, p. 203.

12. Wendell C. Bennett, "The Andean Highlands," *Handbook of South American Indians*, II, 36.

13. Bernabé Cobo, *Historia del nuevo Mundo*, ed. Marcos Jiménez de la Espada (Sevilla, 1892), III, 246-247.

14. Cf. Richard Latcham, *La Existencia de la Propiedad en el antiguo Imperio de los Incas* (Santiago de Chile, 1923), p. 6; Carlos Valdez de la Torre, *Evolución de las Comunidades de Indígenas* (Cuzco, 1921), p. 35; Cunow, *Las Comunidades de Aldea, . . .* p. 31; Louis Baudin, *El Imperio socialista de los Incas*, trans. José Antonio Arze (Santiago de Chile, 1943), p. 185.

15. Jorge Basadre, *Historia del Derecho peruano*, Biblioteca peruana de Ciencias jurídicas y sociales, Vol. I [Lima, 1937], 112.

16. Garcilaso de la Vega, *Comentarios reales de los Incas*, ed. Angel Rosen-

blat (facsimile of edition of 1609 [Buenos Aires, 1943]), Tomo I, Libro V, 225-227.

17. Baudin, p. 177.

18. Valdez de la Torre, p. 38; see also Latcham, p. 44.

19. *Libro primero de los Cabildos de Lima,* deciphered and annotated by E. Torres, P. Patrón, and N. Boloña (Paris, 1900), II, Appendix 3, 184.

20. José María Ots Capdequí, *El Régimen de la Tierra en la América española durante el Periodo colonial* (Ciudad Trujillo, 1946), p. 12.

21. *Libro primero de los Cabildos de Lima,* I, 13.

22. See Julius Klein, *The Mesta: A Study in Spanish Economic History, 1273-1836* (Cambridge, 1920), pp. 239-240; Bailey W. Diffie, *Latin-American Civilization: Colonial Period* (Harrisburg, Pa., 1945), pp. 60-63.

23.. C. H. Haring, *The Spanish Empire in America* (New York, 1947), p. 53.

24. Manuel Belaúnde Guinassi, *La Encomienda en el Perú* (Lima, 1945), p. 25.

25. Cf. Silvio Závala, *New Viewpoints on the Spanish Colonization of America* (Philadelphia, 1943), pp. 80-92.

26. *Libro primero de los Cabildos de Lima,* I, cxxii.

27. Cf. Means, *Fall of the Inca Empire and the Spanish Rule in Peru, 1530-1780* (New York, 1932), pp. 81-96.

28. Belaúnde Guinassi, pp. 112-113.

29. Závala, p. 90.

30. Cf. Haring, pp. 72-73.

31. Considerable confusion has existed on this point, because the term *repartimiento* (distribution) was used in the early period for both land grants and Indian grants. *Encomienda,* however, referred only to the latter. At a later period the term *repartimiento* in New Spain referred to the conscription of Indian labor for special tasks, as well as to the group of laborers thus conscripted. In Peru and other regions *repartimiento* was applied to the forced sale of goods to Indians by their *corregidores.* See F. A. Kirkpatrick, "Repartimiento-Encomienda," *Hispanic-American Historical Review,* XIX (August, 1939), 372-379. See also Závala, pp. 80-92.

32. Fernando de Montesinos, *Anales del Perú—1498-1642* (Madrid, 1906), p. 119.

33. Valdez de la Torre, p. 49.

34. Cf. Félix Cosio, "La Propiedad colectiva del Ayllu," *Revista Universitaria* (Universidad Nacional del Cuzco), Año V, No. 17 (September, 1916), 27.

35. *Relaciones de los Vireyes y Audiencias que han Gobernado el Perú,* I: *Memorial y Ordenanzas de D. Francisco de Toledo* (Lima, 1867), p. 17.

36. *Ibid.,* p. 303.

37. Hildebrando Castro Pozo, "Las Comunidades indígenas del Perú," *Perú en Cifras, 1944-45,* ed. Dario Sainte Marie S. (Buenos Aires, 1945), pp. 164-165.

38. *Cedulario indiano* (facsimile of the edition of 1596 [Madrid, 1945]), folleto 240.

39. *Ibid.*

40. *Recopilación de las Leyes de los Reynos de las Indias* [1680], (facsimile of the edition of 1791 [Madrid, 1943]), II, 43.

41. *Ibid.*

42. *Ibid.,* IV, Titulo XII.

43. Antonio Xavier Pérez López, *Teatro de la Legislación universal de España e Indias* (Madrid, 1793), V, 217-225, reproduced in Ots, pp. 167-174.

44. Ots, p. 114, chaps. ix-x, *passim.*

45. *Recopilación de las Leyes,* . . . IV, Ley X, Titulo XII, 41.

46. Haring, p. 190.

47. *Ibid.,* p. 191.

48. One uncited source, presumably a *Relación anónima* edited by Jiménez de la Espada, places the Peruvian agricultural holdings of the Society of Jesus in 1767 at 203 haciendas of various sizes. (Quoted by Jorge Cornejo Bouroncle, "Las Comunidades Indígenas," *Revista Universitaria* [Universidad Nacional del Cuzco], Año XXXVIII, No. 95 [1948], 84.)

49. Javier Prado, *Estado social del Perú durante la Dominación española* (Lima, 1941), p. 136.

50. Ricardo Bustamante Cisneros, "Las Comunidades de Indígenas en el Perú," *Revista Universitaria* (Universidad Mayor de San Marcos, Lima), Año XIV, I, (2nd trimester, 1919), 451.

51. Bennett, 8 (see above, note 12).

52. Francisco Graña, *La Población del Perú a través de la Historia,* 3rd ed. (Lima, 1940), pp. 2-3.

53. Kubler, noting the great decline of the Indian population during the colonial period, attributes a large part of the losses between 1561 and 1720 to migration from the viceroyalty. The other great depopulating agent was disease, especially smallpox. During this period, Kubler estimates, the Indian population declined approximately half a million. (George Kubler, "The Quechua in the Colonial World," *Handbook of South American Indians,* II, 336-337.)

54. Graña, p. 27.

55. J. Juan and A. de Ulloa, *Noticias secretas de América,* ed. David Barry (London, 1826), Part I, pp. 295-296.

56. *Ibid.,* pp. 524, 673-674.

57. Emilio Romero, *Historia económica del Perú,* Biblioteca de Orientación económica (Buenos Aires, 1949), p. 272.

58. During the colonial period involuntary servitude had been theoretically abolished by the New Laws of 1542, by a royal decree of 1720 ending the *mita,* and by several other government orders, all of which were equally ineffectual.

59. Perú, Ministerio de Trabajo y Asuntos Indígenas, *Legislación indigenista del Perú* (Lima, 1948), p. 11.

60. *Ibid.,* p. 17.

61. *Ibid.*

62. *Ibid.,* pp. 21-22.

63. José Frisancho, "Problemas nacionales: La Propiedad agrícola y el Caciquismo," *Inca,* I, 2 (April-June, 1923), 321-323.

64. Jorge Basadre, *La Multitud, la Ciudad, y el Campo en la Historia del Perú,* Vol. I of Colección de Autores peruanos del Siglo XX, 2nd ed. (Lima, 1947), 233-234.

65. Romero, *Historia económica,* . . . p. 282.

66. Alfredo G. Leubel, *Anuario nacional de 1860* (Lima, 1861), p. 156.

67. Gerardo Klinge, *Política agrícola-alimenticia* (Lima, 1946), pp. 125-126.

68. See p. 122 for a discussion of this election.

3.

1. Based on estimates of the Sociedad Nacional Agraria (S.N.A.), whose figures are: 48,750 hectares in sugar cane and 130,000 hectares in cotton. Sociedad Nacional Agraria, *Memoria, 1948-1949* (Lima, 1949), pp. 33, 52.

2. Carlos M. Alvarez, "El Problema social-económico en el Valle de Chicama" (unpublished bachelor's thesis, Facultad de Derecho, Universidad Nacional de La Libertad, Trujillo, 1949), p. 20.

3. *Ibid.*, pp. 25-38.

4. "Empresa Agrícola 'Chicama' Limitada," *Perú en Cifras 1944-45*, p. 123 (see above, chap. II, note 37).

5. Luis Rose Ugarte, *La Situación alimenticia en el Norte del Perú* (Lima, 1944), pp. 77-78.

6. Perú, Ministerio de Hacienda y Comercio, Dirección nacional de Estadística, *Anuario estadístico del Perú, 1946* (Lima, 1947), pp. 301, 316 (hereinafter cited as *Anuario estadístico*). The total value of exports in 1946 was S/290,583,386. The value of exported sugar and sugar products was S/290,-646,808. The value of exported sugar alone, in 1948, according to the S.N.A., *Memoria, 1948-1949*, was S/223,853,068.

7. The value of cotton exports in 1946 was S/327,749,333, approximately one-third of the total value of all exports. (*Anuario estadístico, 1946*, p. 316.) Cotton export values in 1947 and 1948 were S/224,746,151 and S/277,824,509, respectively (S.N.A., *Memoria, 1948-1949*, p. 47).

8. Rose Ugarte, p. 170.

9. *Anuario estadístico, 1946*, p. 144. The hectarage in 1915 was 24,523; in 1945, it was 59,615. The metric tonnage of rice production in 1915 was 33,300; in 1945, it was 106,282; in 1948, according to the S.N.A. *Memoria, 1948-1949*, the production of 138,000 metric tons was the highest in the country to that time (p. 24).

10. Klinge, *Política agrícola-alimenticia*, pp. 125-126.

11. J. C. Mostajo Chávez, "El Problema agrario en la Provincia de Arequipa" (unpublished bachelor's thesis, Facultad de Derecho, Universidad de San Augustin de Arequipa, 1942). The average-sized unit computed for the same region was 4.03 *topos*.

12. Statement in personal interview by Dr. Francisco Ponce de Leon, Professor of Law, Universidad Nacional del Cuzco, and author of *Al Servicio de los Aborígenes peruanos* (Cuzco, 1946).

13. Rose Ugarte, pp. 28-29.

14. Klinge, "La Agricultura en el Perú," *Perú en Cifras, 1944-45*, p. 72.

15. *Censo nacional, 1940*, I, 68, cuadro 9.

16. This figure for the number of farm families was crudely caculated by dividing the total sierra population (*ibid.*, I, cxlix) by the modal family size (*ibid.*, I, 474-479) and utilizing the information that 52 per cent of the economically active population was devoted to agriculture. In reality this is an extremely conservative estimate, since a much higher percentage of the sierra families is agricultural—at least 60 per cent, with another 15 per cent engaged in ranching enterprises. The point of land scarcity, however, is illustrated by the figures employed.

17. Rómulo Ferrero, *Tierra y Población en el Perú* (Lima, 1938), pp. 13 ff.

18. Carl Brinkmann, "Land Tenure," *Encyclopedia of the Social Sciences,* ed. Edwin R. A. Seligman. Vol. IX (New York, Macmillan, 1944), 73-76.

19. "The Food Situation in Southern Peru," Report of the Economic Division of SCIPA (mimeographed; Lima, 1943), p. 6. (On SCIPA, see above, p. 139.)

4.

1. *Censo nacional,* 1940, I, 368, cuadro 92.
2. W. E. Dunn, *Peru: A Commercial and Industrial Handbook,* U. S. Department of Commerce (Washington, 1925), p. 104.
3. Decreto-Ley No. 11061, 15 de julio, 1949.
4. M. Julio Delgado, "Organización de la Propiedad rural en la Sierra" (unpublished bachelor's thesis, Facultad de Derecho, Universidad Mayor de San Marcos, Lima, 1930).
5. *Anuario estadístico,* 1946, p. 494.
6. César Antonio Ugarte, "La Propiedad agraria en el Perú," *Mercurio Peruano,* Tomo VIII (1922), 901.
7. Ley 10841, 20 de marzo, 1947; Ley 10885, 22 de junio, 1947.
8. *Ibid.*
9. Decreto-Ley No. 33, marzo, 1949.
10. This practice was legally prohibited by a supreme decree, April 1, 1929. According to a recent thesis, it is still practiced in the department of Puno (Julio G. Delgado Aragón, "Macusani" [unpublished bachelor's thesis, Universidad Nacional del Cuzco, 1945]).
11. Cf. Lorgio Vega Gamarra, "El Contrato de Aparcería pecuaria en el Perú" (unpublished bachelor's thesis, Facultad de Derecho, Universidad Mayor de San Marcos, Lima, 1920), *passim.*
12. Delgado, pp. 39-40. Also discussed in Ponce de León, "Sistema de Arrendamiento de Terreños de Cultivo en el Departamento del Cuzco, y el Problema de la Distribución," *Revista Universitaria* (Universidad Nacional del Cuzco), XXII, No. 67, (2nd semester, 1934), pp. 109-140; Romero, *Monografía del Departamento de Puno* (Lima, 1928), pp. 497-498. For *pullan-pura,* see Jorge Isaac Peña, "Algunos Aspectos de Derecho vernacular i las Comunidades de Indígenas del Departamento de Ancash" (unpublished bachelor's thesis, Universidad Nacional de La Libertad, Trujillo, 1947), pp. 15-16.
13. At the time of the study the value of the *sol* varied between five and seven cents of United States dollar.
14. Jorge Gallegos P., "Problemas económico-sociales del Pastor del Altiplano," *La Vida Agrícola,* XXVI, 309 (August, 1949), 645.
15. Carlos Ferdinand Cuadros y Villena, "El 'Arriendo' y la Reforma agraria en la Provincia de la Convención," *Revista Universitaria* (Universidad Nacional del Cuzco), Año XXXVIII, No. 96 (1st semester, 1949), pp. 77-154.
16. "Estudio económico-agropecuaria del Departamento de Cajamarca" (unpublished study by Division of Economic Studies of SCIPA, in cooperation with the Office of Rural Extension of SCIPA in Cajamarca, 1947; mimeographed), p. 8.
17. Hildebrando Castro Pozo, "Las Comunidades indígenas del Perú," p. 172 (see above, chap. II, note 37).
18. Peña (p. 19) notes more or less the same practice in the communities of

the department of Ancash, with the equivalent of *aine*, called *yanapanaqui*, and of *minga*, called *hurganacuy*.

19. Some authors speak of work in *aine*, referring to the system of reciprocal labor (Mishkin, p. 419—see above, chap. I, note 15). M. Julio Delgado speaks of *aine* as the generic term consisting of "the giving of a thing or the loan of a personal service in exchange for the return of the thing or services under equal circumstances." The *minkha* (*minkay*, *minga*) is presented as a special modality of the *aine*, consisting of an exchange of farm work (Delgado, pp. 38-39).

20. Delgado, p. 14; Peña, p. 36.

21. Valdez de la Torre, p. 167 (see above, chap. II, note 14).

5.

1. Moisés Sáenz, *Sobre el Indio peruano y su Incorporación al Medio nacional* (México, D.F., 1933), p. 278.

2. Luis Valcárcel, "La Cuestión agraria en el Cuzco," *Revista Universitaria* (Universidad Nacional del Cuzco), Año III, No. 9 (June, 1914), 21.

3. Manuel González Prada, *Horas de Lucha*, 2nd ed. (Callao, 1924), p. 337.

4. José Carlos Mariátegui, *7 Ensayos de Interpretación de la Realidad peruana*, 2nd ed. (Lima, 1933), p. 25.

5. Estimate based on the study of Leoncio M. Palacios, "Población indígena económicamente activa según el Censo de Población y Ocupación del Año 1940," *Boletín de Estadística Peruana*, Año IX, No. 4 (2nd epoch, October-December, 1948), 87-109.

6. *Censo nacional 1940*, I, p. 189, cuadro 64; p. 152, cuadro 42.

7. *Ibid.*, I, p. 188, cuadro 63.

8. M. H. Kuczynski Godard and C. E. Paz Soldán, *Disección del Indigenismo peruano* (Lima, [1948]), pp. 106-116. Photographic evidence of dietary diseases is given in Kuczynski Godard's *En Orden al Potencial humano del Perú* (Lima, 1949-1950), pp. 92 ff.

9. *Anuario estadístico*, 1946, pp. 70-71.

10. Angélica C. Roncal, "Investigación sobre las Costumbres alimenticias en las Zonas rurales del Perú" (unpublished study by SCIPA, Department of Dietetics and Nutrition, 1947; mimeographed), p. 27.

11. Kuczynski Godard and Paz Soldán, *Disección del Indigenismo peruano*, p. 88.

12. Sáenz, p. 174.

13. Means, "Social Conditions in the Piura-Tumbes Region of Northern Peru," *Scientific Monthly* (November, 1918), pp. 391-392.

14. Francisco Pastor, "El Indígena del Perú: Apuntes para la Sociología nacional," *Revista de la Universidad de Arequipa* (November, 1931), p. 11.

15. Cf. Kuczynski Godard and Paz Soldán, *Disección del Indigenismo peruano*, p. 96.

16. Kuczynski Godard, "Un Latifundio del Sur: Una Contribución al Conocimiento del Problema social," *América Indígena*, VI, 3 (July, 1946), 268.

17. Rowe, "Inca Culture, . . ." p. 330 (see above, chap. II, note 2).

6.

1. Basadre, *Perú: Problema y Posibilidad* (Lima, 1931), p. 162.

2. Among González Prada's more important works should be listed: *Páginas libres* (Paris, 1894), *Anarquía* (Santiago de Chile, 1936), *Bajo el Oprobio* (Paris, 1933), and *Horas de Lucha* (2nd ed., Callao, 1924).

3. Decreto Supremo, 29 de mayo, 1922.

4. Cf. Victor Raúl Haya de la Torre, *Y después de la Guerra, qué?* (Lima, 1946), pp. 223 ff. See also William Rex Crawford, *A Century of Latin American Thought* (Cambridge, Mass., 1944), pp. 188-189.

5. Mariátegui, *7 Ensayos*, p. 34.

6. Carleton Beals, *Fire on the Andes* (Philadelphia, 1934), pp. 419-420.

7. Haya de la Torre, "What Is the A.P.R.A.?" *The Labour Monthly: A Magazine of International Labour,* VIII, No. 12 (December, 1926), 756 ff.

8. Haya de la Torre, *El Antimperialismo y el APRA* (Santiago de Chile, 1936), p. 53.

9. Partido Aprista Peruano, *Manifesto a la Nación,* ed. Manuel Seoane (Buenos Aires, 1932), pp. 57-58.

10. At any rate, these are the impressions gained from Haya's *Y después de la Guerra, qué?*, which stressed a milder "democratic Inter-Americanism without imperialism" (p. 230), and from his *Espacio-Tiempo histórico,* in which he evolves his own historical philosophy. While noting its origins in Hegelian dialectic and Marxist determinism, Haya claims *"the thesis of historical Space-Time asserts, on its part, the dialectical negation of the Marxist philosophy,* taking into account that the conclusions of this doctrine are, also, from their points of observation and reference, exclusively European, viewed and judged from a coordinated or fixed field, from an immovable observation point" (*Espacio-Tiempo histórico* [Lima, 1948], pp. 21-22).

11. To cite a few examples: the establishment of the Banco Agrícola for farm loans, 1931; government regulation of farm tenant contracts by laws of 1946-1947; creation of a Ministry of Agriculture, 1943; state support of agricultural cooperatives through the Ministry of Agriculture; establishment of experimental and extension services by SCIPA since 1943, and by other branches of the Ministry of Agriculture; various irrigation projects; and some few examples of appropriation of haciendas by the goverment for distribution to small farmers.

12. César Antonio Ugarte, *Bosquejo de la Historia económica del Perú* (Lima, 1926), p. 72.

13. Peru, Constitution, Article 47, in *The Constitutions of the Americas,* ed. Russell H. Fitzgibbon (Chicago, 1948).

14. Moisés Poblete Troncoso, *Condiciones de Vida y de Trabajo de la Población indígena del Perú,* Estudios y Documentos, Serie B., No. 28 (Ginebra, 1938), p. 100.

15. C. W. Sutton, "Irrigation in Peru," *Andean Air Mail and Peruvian Times,* VIII, 402 (September 3, 1948), 8-9.

16. *Ibid.*

17. Klinge, *Política agrícola-alimenticia,* p. 312 (see above, chap. II, note 67).

18. Mario del Río, *La Inmigración y su Desarrollo en el Perú* (Lima, 1929), *passim.*

19. J. Alberto Barreda, "El Desarrollo de la Colonización en Tingo María," *La Vida Agrícola,* XXVII, 317 (April, 1950), 289-296.

20. According to the *Memoria* of the Bank for 1947-1948, losses through seventeen seasons of operation amounted to only 0.063 per cent of the total loans made. Losses on S/437,599,969.39 loaned were approximately S/2,-750,000. The loans made to small farmers (those under 10,000 *soles*) showed a much higher loss rate than the general average, being 0.95 per cent. (Banco Agrícola del Perú, *Memoria, 1947-1948* [Lima, 1949].)

21. In the 1947-1948 year, 5,732 loans were made, totaling S/62,051,-642.69. Of these, 516 were to large agriculturists and accounted for S/45,120,-906.44; the remainder of the loans (5,216) were to small farmers and amounted to S/16,930,736.25. (Information supplied by the directorate of the Banco Agrícola.)

22. Francisco Alvariño Herr, "Origen del Movimiento cooperativo en el Perú," *El Movimiento cooperativo en las Américas* (Montreal, 1943), p. 49.

23. Sáenz, *Sobre el Indio peruano*, . . . (see above, chap. V, note 1), pp. 81-82; Castro Pozo, *Nuestra Comunidad Indígena* (Lima, 1924), pp. 63-68; Harry Tschopik, *Highland Communities of Central Peru: A Regional Survey*, Smithsonian Institution, Institute of Social Anthropology, Publication No. 5 (Washington, 1947), p. 48.

24. Tschopik, *loc. cit.* This passage also illustrates the return of lands formerly held in mortmain to the villagers themselves; see *supra*, p. 79.

25. See Watt Stewart, *Henry Meiggs, Yankee Pizarro* (Durham, N. C., 1936), for an account of Meiggs's experiences in constructing the early railroads of Peru.

26. *Anuario estadístico, 1946*, p. 216.

27. Carlos Moreyra y Paz Soldán, "Las Comunicaciones y los Transportes en el Perú," *Perú en Cifras, 1944-45*, pp. 377-393 (see above, chap. II, note 37).

28. Ley orgánica de Educación Pública, 1 de abril, 1941.

29. *Anuario estadístico, 1946*, pp. 572-573, 580-581.

30. "Educación rural," *El Nuevo Educador*, Año VI, No. 8 (May, 1950), 45.

31. The Institute of American Affairs was placed under the Technical Cooperation Administration in 1950 as part of the Point Four Program. The T.C.A. later came under the jurisdiction of the Mutual Security Agency, and in 1953 became part of the Foreign Operations Administration organized in that year.

32. Klinge, "La Agricultura en el Perú," p. 90 (see above, chap. III, note 14).

33. This information has been drawn largely from an unpublished report of the Director of the Food Production in Peru to the Institute of Inter-American Affairs (1948), and from *Informaciones del SCIPA*, a quarterly publication of the organization.

34. *Supra*, p. 130.

35. Perú, Ministerio de Agricultura, Dirección de Colonización y Asuntos Orientales, *La Acción oficial en el Desarrollo agropecuario de la Colonización de Tingo María, Años 1942-1946* (Lima, 1947), pp. 157-159.

Bibliography

Books

BASADRE, JORGE. *Historia del Derecho peruano.* Vol. I of Biblioteca peruana de Ciencias jurídicas y sociales. Lima: Editorial Antena, S.A., 1937.
————. *La Multitud, la Ciudad, y el Campo en la Historia del Perú.* Vol. I of Colección de Autores peruanos del Siglo XX. 2nd ed. Lima: Editorial Huascarán, S.A., 1947.
————. *Perú: Problema y Posibilidad.* Lima: Biblioteca Peruana, 1931.
BAUDIN, LOUIS. *El Imperio socialista de los Incas.* Translated by José Antonio Arze. Santiago de Chile: Empresa Editorial Zig-Zag, 1943.
BEALS, CARLETON. *Fire on the Andes.* Philadelphia: J. B. Lippincott, 1934.
BELAÚNDE GUINASSI, MANUEL. *La Encomienda en el Perú.* Lima: Editorial Mercurio Peruano, 1945.
BOWMAN, ISAIAH. *The Andes of Southern Peru: Geographical Reconnaissance along the Seventy-third Meridian.* New York: Henry Holt and Co., 1916.
CASTRO POZO, HILDEBRANDO. *Nuestra Comunidad Indígena.* Lima: Editorial El Lucero, 1924.
COBO, BERNABÉ. *Historia del nuevo Mundo.* 4 vols. Edited by Marcos Jiménez de la Espada. Sevilla: Imprenta de E. Rasco, 1890-95.
CRAWFORD, WILLIAM REX. *A Century of Latin American Thought.* Cambridge: Harvard University Press, 1944.
CUNOW, HEINRICH. *Las Comunidades de Aldea y de Marca del Perú antiguo.* Translated from the German by María Woitscheck. Paris: Imprimerie Le Moil et Pascaly, 1929.
————. *La Organización social del Imperio de los Incas.* Translated by María Woitscheck. Lima: Editorial Libreria Peruana, 1933.
DIFFIE, BAILEY W. *Latin-American Civilization: Colonial Period.* Harrisburg, Pa.: Stackpole Sons, 1945.
DUNN, W. E. *Peru: a Commercial and Industrial Handbook,* U.S. Department of Commerce. Washington: U.S. Government Printing Office, 1925.
FERRERO, RÓMULO. *Tierra y Población en el Perú.* Lima: Banco Agrícola del Perú, 1938.
FITZGIBBON, RUSSELL H. (ed.). *The Constitutions of the Americas.* Chicago: University of Chicago Press, 1948.
GARCILASO DE LA VEGA. *Comentarios reales de los Incas.* 2 vols. Edited by Angel Rosenblat. Facsimile of the edition of 1609. Buenos Aires: Emecé Editores, 1943.

163

164 — MAN AND LAND IN PERU

GERBI, ANTONELLO. *El Perú en Marcha*. Lima: Banco de Credito del Perú, 1943.

GONZÁLEZ PRADA, MANUEL. *Anarquía*. Santiago de Chile: Ediciones Ercilla, 1936.

————. *Bajo el Oprobio*. Paris: Tip. de L. Bellenand et Fils, 1933.

————. *Horas de Lucha*. 2nd ed. Callao: Tipografía "LUX," 1924.

————. *Páginas libres*. Paris: Tip. de P. Dupont, 1894.

GRAÑA, FRANCISCO. *La Población del Perú a través de la Historia*. 3rd ed. Lima: Imprenta Torres Aguirre, 1940.

HANKE, LEWIS. *The Spanish Struggle for Justice in the Conquest of America*. Philadelphia: University of Pennsylvania Press, 1949.

HARING, C. H. *The Spanish Empire in America*. New York: Oxford University Press, 1947.

HAYA DE LA TORRE, VICTOR RAÚL. *El Antimperialismo y el APRA*. Santiago de Chile: Ediciones Ercilla, 1936.

————. *Espacio-Tiempo histórico*. Lima, 1948.

————. *Y después de la Guerra, qué?* Lima: Editorial PCTM, 1946.

JAMES, PRESTON E. *Latin America*. Revised edition. New York: Odyssey Press, 1950.

JUAN, JORGE, and ULLOA, A. DE. *Noticias secretas de América*. Edited by David Barry. London: Imprenta de R. Taylor, 1826.

KLEIN, JULIUS. *The Mesta: A Study in Spanish Economic History, 1273-1836*. Cambridge: Harvard University Press, 1920.

KLINGE, GERARDO. *Política agrícola-alimenticia*. Lima: Imprenta Torres Aguirre, S.A., 1946.

KUCZYNSKI GODARD, MAXIME H. *En Orden al Potencial humano del Perú*. Lima: Comisión Ejecutiva del Inventario del Potencial Económico de la Nación. Fascículo segundo, 1949-1950.

KUCZYNSKI GODARD, M. H., and PAZ SOLDÁN, C. E. *Disección del Indigenismo peruano*. Lima: Instituto de Medicina Social [1948].

LATCHAM, RICHARD. *La Existencia de la Propiedad en el antiguo Imperio de los Incas*. Santiago de Chile: Imprenta i Litografía Universo, 1923.

LEUBEL, ALFREDO G. *Anuario nacional de 1860*. Lima: Imprenta del "Comercio," 1861.

MARIÁTEGUI, JOSÉ CARLOS. *7 Ensayos de Interpretación de la Realidad peruana*. 2nd ed. Lima: Biblioteca "Amauta," 1933.

MEANS, PHILIP AINSWORTH. *Ancient Civilizations of the Andes*. New York: Charles Scribner's Sons, 1942.

————. *Fall of the Inca Empire and the Spanish Rule in Peru, 1530-1780*. New York: Charles Scribner's Sons, 1932.

MEJÍA VALERA, JOSÉ. *Organización de la Sociedad en el Perú precolombino, hasta la Aparición del Estado Inka*. Lima: Enrique Bustamante y Ballivién, Sucesor, 1946.

MONTESINOS, FERNANDO DE. *Anales del Perú—1498-1642*. Madrid: Víctor M. Maurtua, 1906.

OTS CAPDEQUÍ, JOSÉ MARÍA. *El Régimen de la Tierra en la América española durante el Periodo colonial*. Ciudad Trujillo: Editora Montalvo, 1946.

PAREJA PAZ SOLDÁN, JOSÉ. *Geografía del Perú*. 2nd ed. Lima: D. Miranda, 1943.

PAZ SOLDÁN, C. E. See under Kuczynski.

PÉREZ LÓPEZ, ANTONIO XAVIER. *Teatre de la Legislación universal de España e Indias.* Vol. V. Madrid, 1793.

POBLETE TRONCOSO, MOISÉS. *Condiciones de Vida y de Trabajo de la Población indígena del Perú.* Estudios y Documentos, Serie B, No. 28. Ginebra: Oficina Internacional del Trabajo, 1938.

PONCE DE LEÓN, FRANCISCO. *Al Servicio de los Aborígenes peruanos.* Cuzco: Librería y Imprenta D. Miranda, 1946.

PRADO, JAVIER. *Estado social del Perú durante la Dominación española.* Lima: Librería y Imprenta Gil, 1941.

RELACIÓN ANÓNIMA. Edited by Marcus Jiménez de la Espada, 1767.

RÍO, MARIO DEL. *La Inmigración y su Desarrollo en el Perú.* Lima: Sanmartí y Cía., 1929.

ROMERO, EMILIO. *Geografía económica del Perú.* Lima: Imprenta Torres Aguirre, 1939.

―――. *Historia económica del Perú.* Biblioteca de Orientación económica. Buenos Aires: Editorial Sudamericana, 1949.

―――. *Monografía del Departamento de Puno.* Lima: Imprenta Torres Aguirre, 1928.

ROSE UGARTE, LUIS. *La Situación alimenticia en el Norte del Perú.* Lima: Ministerio de Agricultura, SCIPA, 1944.

―――. *La Situación alimenticia en el Perú.* Lima: Ministerio de Agricultura, SCIPA, 1945.

SAAVEDRA, BAUTISTA. *El Ayllu.* 2nd ed. Santiago de Chile: Editorial Nascimiento, 1938.

SÁENZ, MOISÉS. *Sobre el Indio peruano y su Incorporación al Medio nacional.* México, D.F.: Secretaria de Educación Pública, 1933.

SIMPSON, LESLEY BYRD. *The Economienda in New Spain: Forced Native Labor in the Spanish Colonies, 1492-1550.* Berkeley: University of California Press, 1929.

STEWART, WATT. *Henry Meiggs, Yankee Pizarro.* Durham, N.C.: Duke University Press, 1946.

TELLO, JULIO C. *Origen y Desarrollo de las Civilizaciones prehistóricas andinas.* Lima: Librería y Imprenta Gil, S.A., 1942.

TSCHOPIK, HARRY. *Highland Communities of Central Peru: A Regional Survey.* Smithsonian Institution, Institute of Social Anthropology, Publication No. 5. Washington: U.S. Government Printing Office, 1947.

UGARTE, CÉSAR ANTONIO. *Bosquejo de la Historia económica del Perú.* Lima: Imprenta Cabieses, 1926.

UHLE, MAX. *Las antiguas Civilizaciones de Manta.* Quito: Escuela Tipográfica Salesiaro, 1931.

UNITED NATIONS. *Demographic Yearbook, 1951.* New York: Statistical Office of the United Nations, 1952.

URIEL GARCIA, J. *El nuevo Indio.* Cuzco: Editorial H. G. Rozas, Sucesores, 1930.

URTEAGA, HORATIO. *El Imperio incaico en el que se incluye la Historial del Ayllu y Familia de los Incas.* Lima: Librería y Imprenta Gil, S.A., 1931.

VALDEZ DE LA TORRE, CARLOS. *Evolución de las Comunidades de Indígenas.* Cuzco: Editorial Euforion, 1921.

ZÁVALA, SILVIO. *New Viewpoints on the Spanish Colonization of America.* Philadelphia: University of Pennsylvania Press, 1934.

Public Documents

Cedulario indiano. Facsimile of the edition of 1596. Folleto No. 240. Madrid: Editorial Cultura Hispanica, 1945.

Leyes de Indias. Vol. IV. 3rd ed. Madrid: Imprenta "Sáenz Hermanos," 1935.

Las Leyes Nuevas, 1542-1543. Transcribed and annotated by Antonio Muro Orejón. Facsimile edition. Sevilla: Consejo Superior de Investigaciones Cientificas, Escuela de Estudios Hispano-Americanas de la Universidad de Sevilla, 1945.

Libro primero de los Cabildos de Lima. Deciphered and annotated by E. Torres, P. Patrón, and N. Boloña. Paris: Imprimerie Paul DuPont, 1900.

PERÚ. Ministerio de Agricultura. Dirección de Colonización y Asuntos Orientales. *La Acción oficial en el Desarrollo agropecuario de la Colonización de Tingo María, Años 1942-1946*. Lima: Ministerio de Agricultura, 1947.

PERÚ. Ministerio de Hacienda y Comercio. Dirección nacional de Estadística. *Anuario estadístico del Perú, 1946*. Lima: Imprenta Torres Aguirre, 1947.

————. *Censo nacional de Población y Ocupación, 1940*. Vol. I: *Resúmenes generales*. Lima: Imprenta Torres Aguirre, 1944.

PERÚ. Ministerio de Trabajo y Asuntos Indígenas. *Legislación indigenista del Perú*. Lima: Dirección General de Asuntos Indígenas, 1948.

Recopilación de las Leyes de los Reynos de las Indias [1680]. Facsimile of the edition of 1791. Madrid, 1943.

Relaciones de los Vireyes y Audiencias que han Gobernado el Perú. Vol. I: *Memorial y Ordenanzas de D. Francisco de Toledo*. Lima: Imprenta del Estado, 1867.

Reports

BANCO AGRÍCOLA DEL PERÚ. *Memoria, 1947-1948*. Lima: Librería y Imprenta Gil, S.A., 1949.

————. *Memorias del Banco, Ejercicios anuales 1° al 15°*. Lima: Imprenta Torres Aguirre, S.A., 1947.

PARTIDO APRISTA PERUANO. *Manifesto a la Nación*. Edited by Manuel Seoane. Buenos Aires: Editorial "La Vanguardia," 1932.

SOCIEDAD NACIONAL AGRARIA. *Memoria, 1948-1949*. Lima: Librería y Imprenta Gil, S.A., 1949.

Articles

ALVARIÑO HERR, FRANCISCO. "Origen del Movimiento cooperativo en el Perú," *El Movimiento cooperativo en las Américas*. Montreal: Oficina Internacional del Trabajo, 1943, p. 49.

BARREDA, J. ALBERTO. "El Desarrollo de la Colonización en Tingo María," *La Vida Agrícola*, XXVII, 317 (April, 1950), 289-296.

BENNETT, WENDELL C. "The Andean Highlands," *The Andean Civilizations*. Vol. II of *Handbook of South American Indians*. Smithsonian Institution, Bureau of American Ethnology, Bulletin 143. Washington: U.S. Government Printing Office, 1946. Pp. 1-60.

BRINKMANN, CARL. "Land Tenure," *Encyclopedia of the Social Sciences*. Vol. IX. (New York: The Macmillan Co., 1944), 73-76.

BUSTAMANTE CISNEROS, RICARDO. "Las Comunidades de Indígenas en el Perú," *Revista Universitaria* (Universidad Mayor de San Marcos, Lima), Año XIV, I (2nd trimester, 1919), 433-488.

CASTRO POZO, HILDEBRANDO. "Las Comunidades indígenas del Perú," *Perú en Cifras, 1944-45*. Edited by Dario Sainte Marie S. Buenos Aires: Ediciones Internacionales, 1945, pp. 158-174.

CORNEJO BOURONCLE, JORGE. "Las Comunidades Indígenas," *Revista Universitaria* (Universidad Nacional del Cuzco), Año XXXVIII, No. 95 (1948), pp. 67-129.

COSIO, FÉLIX. "La Propiedad colectiva del Ayllu," *Revista Universitaria* (Universidad Nacional del Cuzco), Año V, No. 17 (September, 1916), pp. 10-42.

CUADROS Y VILLENA, CARLOS FERDINAND. "El 'Arriendo' y la Reforma agraria en la Provincia de la Convención," *Revista Universitaria* (Universidad Nacional del Cuzco), Año XXXVIII, No. 96 (1st semester, 1949), pp. 77-154.

"Educación rural," *El Nuevo Educador*, Año VI, No. 8 (May, 1950), p. 45.

"Empresa Agrícola 'Chicama' Limitada," *Perú en Cifras, 1944-45*. Edited by Dario Sainte Marie S. Buenos Aires: Ediciones Internacionales, 1945, pp. 121-130.

FRISANCHO, JOSÉ. "Problemas nacionales: La Propiedad agrícola y el Caciquismo," *Inca*, I, 2 (April-June, 1923), 321-328.

GALLEGOS P., JORGE. "Problemas económico-sociales del Pastor del Altiplano," *La Vida Agrícola*, XXVI, 309 (August, 1949), 635-650.

"Haciendas 'Cartavio' y 'Paramonga,'" *Perú en Cifras, 1944-45*. Edited by Dario Sainte Marie S. Buenos Aires: Ediciones Internacionales, 1945, pp. 131-132.

HAYA DE LA TORRE, VICTOR RAÚL. "What is the A.P.R.A.?" *The Labour Monthly: A Magazine of International Labour*, VIII, 12 (December, 1926), 756-759.

KIRKPATRICK, F. A. "Repartimiento-Encomienda," *Hispanic-American Historical Review*, XIX (August, 1939), 372-379.

KLINGE, GERARDO. "La Agricultura en el Perú," *Perú en Cifras, 1944-45*. Edited by Dario Sainte Marie S. Buenos Aires: Ediciones Internacionales, 1945, pp. 65-94.

KUBLER, GEORGE. "The Quechua in the Colonial World," *The Andean Civilizations*. Vol. II of *Handbook of South American Indians*, Smithsonian Institution, Bureau of American Ethnology, Bulletin 143. Washington: U.S. Government Printing Office, 1946, pp. 331-410.

KUCZYNSKI GODARD, MAXIME H. "Un Latifundio del Sur: Una Contribución al Conocimiento del Problema social," *América Indígena*, VI, 3 (July, 1946), pp. 257-274.

LABARTHE, GODOFREDO. "La Ganadería en el Perú," *Perú en Cifras, 1944-45*. Edited by Dario Sainte Marie S. Buenos Aires: Ediciones Internacionales, 1945, pp. 136-146.

MEANS, PHILIP AINSWORTH. "Social Conditions in the Piura-Tumbes Region of Northern Peru," *Scientific Monthly* (November, 1918), pp. 385-399.

MISHKIN, BERNARD. "The Contemporary Quechua," *The Andean Civilizations*. Vol. II of *Handbook of South American Indians*. Smithsonian Institution, Bureau of American Ethnology, Bulletin 143. Washington: U.S. Government Printing Office, 1946, pp. 411-470.

MOREYRA Y PAZ SOLDÁN, CARLOS. "Las Comunicaciones y los Transportes en el Perú," *Perú en Cifras, 1944-45*. Edited by Dario Sainte Marie S. Buenos Aires: Ediciones Internacionales, 1945, pp. 377-393.

PAJUELO VERA, JOSÉ A. "La Ganadería comunal indígena en el País," *La Vida Agrícola*, XXV, 30 (December, 1948), 1071-1082.

PALACIOS, LEONCIO M. "Población indígena económicamente activa según el Censo de Población y Ocupacíon del Año 1940," *Boletín de Estadística Peruana*, Año IX, No. 4 (2nd epoch, October-December, 1948), 87-109.

PASTOR, FRANCISCO. "El Indígena del Perú: Apuntes para la Sociología nacional," *Revista de la Universidad de Arequipa* (November, 1931), pp. 64-75.

PAULET, PEDRO E. "Los cinco Regiones del Perú," *Peruanidad*, I, 1 (November, 1941), 5-12.

PONCE DE LEÓN, FRANCISCO. "Sistema de Arrendamiento de Terreños de Cultivo en el Departamento del Cuzco, y el Problema de la Distribución," *Revista Universitaria* (Universidad Nacional del Cuzco), XXII, 67 (2nd semester, 1934), 109-140.

PULGAR VIDAL, JAVIER. "Las ocho Regiones naturales del Perú," *Boletín del Museo de Historia natural "Javier Prado,"* V, 17 (2nd trimester, 1941), 145-160.

ROMERO, EMILIO. "Caciquismo," *Revista de Economia y Finanzas*, VI (November, 1935), 265-266.

ROWE, JOHN H. "Inca Culture at the Time of the Spanish Conquest," *The Andean Civilizations*. Vol. II of *Handbook of South American Indians*. Smithsonian Institution, Bureau of American Ethnology, Bulletin 143, Washington: U.S. Government Printing Office, 1946, 183-330.

SUTTON, C. W. "Irrigation in Peru," *Andean Air Mail and Peruvian Times*, VIII, 402 (September 3, 1948), 8-9.

UGARTE, CÉSAR ANTONIO. "La Política agraria de la República," *Mercurio Peruano*, Tomo X (1923), 664-671.

————. "La Propriedad agraria en el Perú," *Mercurio Peruano*, Tomo VIII (1922), 891-907.

UHLE, MAX. "Desarrollo y Origen de las Civilizaciones americanas" (reprint from *Proceedings of the Twentv-third International Congress of Americanists*), September, 1928.

VALCÁRCEL, LUIS. "La Cuestión agraria en el Cuzco," *Revista Universitaria* (Universidad Nacional del Cuzco), Año III, No. 9 (June, 1914), 19-35.

WHITE, C. LANGDON, "Rumblings over the Andes," *The Pacific Spectator*, III, 4 (Autumn, 1949), 403-420.

Unpublished Material

ALVAREZ, CARLOS M. "El Problema social-económico en el Valle de Chicama." Bachelor's thesis, Facultad de Derecho, Universidad Nacional de La Libertad, Trujillo, 1949.

"Balance del Comercio exterior de Productos alimenticios del Perú, Año 1949." Lima: SCIPA, June, 1950 (mimeographed).

DELGADO, M. JULIO. "Organización de la Propiedad rural en la Sierra." Bachelor's thesis, Facultad de Derecho, Universidad Mayor de San Marcos, Lima, 1930.

DELGADO ARAGÓN, JULIO G. "Macusani." Bachelor's thesis, Universidad Nacional del Cuzco, 1945.

"Estudio económico-agropecuario del Departamento de Cajamarca." Study by the Division of Economic Studies of SCIPA, in cooperation with the Office of Rural Extension of SCIPA in Cajamarca, 1947 (mimeographed).

"The Food Situation in Southern Peru." Report of the Economic Division of SCIPA. Lima: SCIPA, 1943 (mimeographed).

MOSTAJO CHAVEZ, J. C. "El problema agrario en la Provincia de Arequipa." Bachelor's thesis, Facultad de Derecho, Universidad de San Augustin de Arequipa, 1942.

NEALE, JOHN R. "Peru." Report of the Director of the Food Production Mission in Peru to the Institute of Inter-American Affairs, Washington, 1948.

PEÑA, JORGE ISAAC. "Algunos Aspectos de Derecho vernacular i las Comunidades de Indígenas del Departamento de Ancash." Bachelor's thesis, Universidad Nacional de La Libertad, Trujillo, 1947.

RONCAL, ANGÉLICA C. "Investigación sobre las Costumbres alimenticias en las Zonas rurales del Perú." Study by SCIPA, Department of Dietetics and Nutrition, 1947 (mimeographed).

"Valor de la Mano de Obra en los diferentes Valles de la República." Lima: Ministerio de Agricultura, 1949 (mimeographed).

VEGA GAMARRA, LORGIO. "El Contrato de Aparcería pecuaria en el Perú." Bachelor's thesis, Facultad de Derecho, Universidad Mayor de San Marcos, Lima, 1920.

Legal References

Ley 2285, 16 de octubre, 1916.
Constitución de 1920, Título IV, Artículos 41 y 58.
Decreto supremo, 29 de mayo, 1922.
Ley orgánica de Educación Pública, 1 de abril, 1941.
Decreto supremo, No. 326, 27 de junio, 1941.
Ley 10841, 20 de marzo, 1947.
Ley 10885, 22 de junio, 1947.
Decreto-Ley No. 33, marzo, 1949.
Decreto-Ley No. 11061, 15 de julio, 1949.
Decreto-Ley No. 11330, 21 de abril, 1950.

Index